OZZIE
SWEET

"THE BOYS OF SPRING"

Timeless Portraits from the Grapefruit League, 1947-2005

Text by Larry Canale | *Foreword by Frank Robinson*

SPORT CLASSIC BOOKS

Published in the United States of America by Sport Media Publishing Inc.,
Wilmington, Delaware, and simultaneously in Canada.

For information about permission to reproduce selections from this book,
please write to:
Permissions
Sport Media Publishing, Inc.,
21 Carlaw Ave.,
Toronto, Ontario, Canada, M4M 2R6
www.sportclassicbooks.com

All photographs by Ozzie Sweet except:

Pages 5; 14 (top, left); 207; 208; and 209, by Larry Canale. Page 12, by Jim Pond. Page 14 (third from left), by Diane Sweet. Page 14 (far right), by Ozzie's Aunt Edna. Page 14 (second from left), by Lauren Canale. Page 14 (bottom), by Nick Scutti.

Photographs © Ozzie Sweet except for the following:

Grateful acknowledgment is made to ESPN for permission to reproduce the following:

Page 19 (bottom, Floyd Patterson); page 24 (top, Joe DiMaggio); pages 50 and 51 (Casey Stengel); page 65 (Johnny Bench); page 133 (Frank Robinson); page 134 (Al Rosen); page 158 (Carl Yastrzemski); page 176 (Bob Lemon); page 198 (Mudcat Grant); page 200 (Minnie Minoso); page 211 (Yankees); and page 228 (Maury Wills, center and right).

The following photographs are presented via the kind courtesy of Randall Swearingen of Mickey-Mantle.com:

Page 18 (Mickey Mantle, bottom); pages 62-63 (Mickey Mantle, Billy Martin); page 125 (Ted Kluszewski); page 126 (Mickey Mantle, bottom); page 143 (Mickey Mantle); page 148 (Pete Rose); pages 152 and 153 (Frank Robinson); and page 171 (Sandy Koufax).

Newsweek covers on page 17 courtesy of Newsweek Inc. ©1947.

Time and *Sports Illustrated* covers on page 17 courtesy of Time Inc. ©1954 and ©1991.

Boys' Life cover on page 64 courtesy of Boys' Life ©1969.

SPORT covers on page 18 courtesy Sport Media Enterprises Inc.

This book is set in Scala. Captions are Trade Gothic.

Cover design: Paul Hodgson
Interior design and layout: Paul Hodgson
Photo work: Peter Grucza, Greg Oliver, Eddie Chau and Jones & Morris Photo Digital Imaging

ISBN: 1-894963-39-3

Library of Congress Control Number: 2004116200

Printed in Canada

DEDICATION

To my wife Diane, my daughters Pamela and
Linnea, and my son Blair. Thank you for the
love and support—and creative input—through
the years. *OZZIE SWEET*

To my family, especially the sunniest, most
smiling faces I know, my lovable little
daughters Quinlyn and Karsyn. This one's
for you. *LARRY CANALE*

ACKNOWLEDGEMENTS
Ozzie Sweet and I owe thanks
and appreciation to many
people who provided help to us
in a variety of ways.

First, thanks to the countless
baseball media relations
professionals who offered
access to the game's brightest
names and faces over the years.
Special thanks to those who
helped us add current images
to this book—especially Rick
Cerrone of the New York
Yankees, Warren Miller of the
Houston Astros, and Jim
Trdinich of the Pittsburgh
Pirates.

Great photographs need great
subjects, so thanks are due, of
course, to all of the ballplayers
over the years who cooperated
with Ozzie. Special thanks to
Frank Robinson for his
involvement with *The Boys of*

Spring. We'd like to extend
thanks to the Baseball Hall of
Fame Museum & Library,
especially Ted Spencer, vice-
president and chief curator; Pat
Kelly, photo archivist; Greg
Harris, director of development;
and Freddy Berowski, Claudette
Burke, and Bill Francis of the
A. Bartlett Giamatti Research
Center at the Hall of Fame. We
also appreciate the help of
Richard Johnson, curator of The
Sports Museum of New
England.

Thanks to the great
photographers who approached
Ozzie at spring training in 2003
'04, and '05 to share their
appreciation, especially Rich
Pilling of Major League
Baseball and Chuck Solomon of
Sports Illustrated as well as
Victor Baldizon, Tim Cammett,
Chip Carter, Tom DiPace, Larry

Kinchen, and Jon Soo Hoo.
Thanks also to photography
legends Neil Leifer and Walter
Iooss for their support and
cooperation. Ozzie thanks his
longtime assistants, Pete
Brown, John Messmore, and
Nick Scutti, who contributed so
much behind-the-scenes help
on many of those old baseball
photo shoots, as well as
Michelle LeBlanc and Jane
Sawyer.

Thanks to the many people
who offered advice and
feedback to Ozzie and me:
Marty Appel, Dave Baudouin,
Kelly Carlie, Nik Kleinberg,
Simeon Lipman, Dan Muse,
Bob Ryan, Chuck Stallings, Dan
Sullivan, Phil Wood, and, of
course, Lauren Canale, Larry
and Millie Canale, Diane Sweet,
Pamela Sweet, Linnea Sweet,
Peter Fairfield, and Blair Sweet.

Very special thanks to Mark
Durand of ESPN for his
cooperation in sharing a
number of the photographer's
images with the readers of this
book. Likewise, we thank
Randall Swearingen of
www.mickey-mantle.com and
The Mickey Mantle Museum for
sharing several more of the
photographer's images.

Finally, we owe a great deal
of thanks to Wayne Parrish, Jim
O'Leary, Peter Grucza, and Greg
Oliver of Sport Media
Publishing for making this book
a reality and to designer Paul
Hodgson for creating such an
ideal setting for Ozzie's
photography. We envisioned *The
Boys of Spring* as a positive,
happy place for baseball fans to
visit; thank you for the care you
put into these pages to make it
happen.   —*L.C.*

CONTENTS

ROAD WARRIOR

Each spring, Ozzie Sweet would cram his Buick Woody station wagon full of his cameras, lights and other paraphernalia before hitting the road for Florida. That's Ozzie in the white hat, with his assistant Nick Scutti, and the family pet in this 1950s photo.

Previous pages

Page 1

Laundry day at the Washington Senators' camp, 1969.

Page 2 and 3

The Houston Astros arrive for work in 2004. The high uniform numbers indicate these are mainly rookies, with a sprinkling of journeymen. During the season ahead, though, several would make an impact for the Astros. Among them: pitcher Brad Lidge (No. 54), who emerged as a dominant closer, and Jose Vizcaino (No. 10), who became the starting shortstop. John Buck (No. 67) became the Royals starting catcher after a July trade.

Page 4

The unique uncovered dugouts at Dodgertown in Vero Beach are showcased in this 1982 shot. Note that Ozzie has caught the eye of Minnesota rookie Frank Viola, seated near the middle of the visiting Twins' bench.

THE THROWBACK PHOTOGRAPHER
BY FRANK ROBINSON

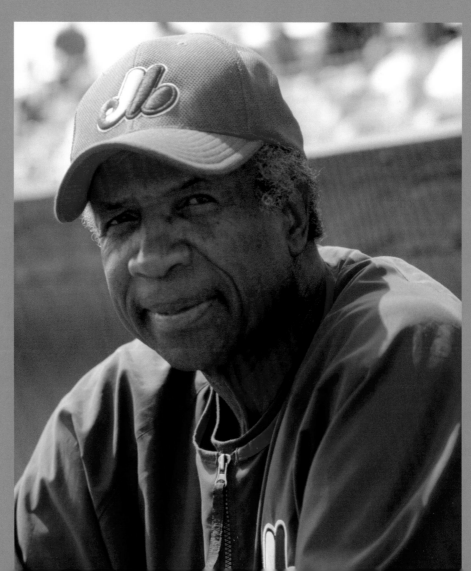

It took me a moment to realize who he was, this familiar face with the camera in his hands. I had just walked into our dugout one hot afternoon in March 2003, ready for the first pitch of an Expos spring training game. As I was looking over the lineup card, I heard, "Hi, Frank. Do you remember me? I'm Ozzie Sweet."

Well, like I said, it took me a moment, but of course I remember. Ozzie was a regular at spring training in the 1950s, when I first came up to the big leagues with the Cincinnati Redlegs (as they were called from 1953 through 1958) and in the 1960s, when I played with the Reds and later the Baltimore Orioles. During that era, Ozzie was an energetic photographer who stood out from the rest. He always had a creative idea for a picture—a different way to pose us, or unusual props, or a unique setting.

Of course, posing for a portrait isn't usually a fun thing to do, but Ozzie had a way of making it painless. He'd arrange a photo shoot and then go to great lengths to have everything set up—his lights, the backdrop, bats, and all that photography equipment. While he'd work, he'd toss around a corny joke or two to lighten things up and distract us from the camera. Most important, he'd work quickly. Ballplayers always appreciated that, because sitting for a photographer—even Ozzie Sweet—left us as sitting ducks for our teammates' pranks and needling.

Ozzie photographed me at spring training several times during my years with Cincinnati between 1956 and '65 and again during my years with the Orioles. But those days were a long time ago, so when Ozzie turned up at our Montreal Expos camp in Melbourne, Fla., in 2003, it was a surprise for me, as it would have been for anyone who met up with an old acquaintance he hadn't seen in several decades. So I said hello to Ozzie and shook his hand—and then he asked a question that was anything but surprising: "Do you mind if I take a few new photographs of you for a spring training book?"

The game was literally a minute or two from starting, but how could I say no? I told him to go ahead and asked what he wanted me to do.

"Just keep doing what you were doing," he said. And he pointed his camera at me for the first time since the late 1960s.

A year later, in March 2004, guess who shows up at camp again.... Yep, ol' Ozzie, back at spring training. This time, I wasn't so surprised. In fact, I expect to see him down here next year, and the year after, and the year after.... I don't blame Ozzie. Spring training is, after all, a great place to be, and I speak from experience. I've been coming to spring training since 1954. That's 50 spring trainings I've enjoyed—first as a minor leaguer, then as a big leaguer, then as a player/manager, then as a manager, then as a league official, and then as a manager again. I'll never get tired of it, and I don't think Ozzie will either.

It's been great to catch up with Ozzie Sweet, who's obviously one of the brightest stars in his field. His work, especially on those old *SPORT* magazine covers in the 1950s and '60s, was always recognizable—always sharp and true. Baseball history certainly has been enriched by Ozzie's talent and imagination, and we're fortunate that he's still hard at work. It's inspiring to see him behind his camera again, still capturing the images of this great game after all these years.

See you next spring, Ozzie.

FRANK ROBINSON, 2005

Frank Robinson, one of Ozzie's favorite subjects, played 21 years for the Reds, Orioles, Dodgers, Angels, and Indians. A first-ballot Hall of Fame inductee in 1982, he hit 586 home runs and batted .294 with 2,943 hits, 1,829 runs, and 1,812 RBI. He's the only player to win MVP awards in both the National and American leagues: 1961 in the NL and 1966 (when he won the Triple Crown) in the AL. He has served as manager of the Indians, Giants, Orioles, and Expos/Nationals, and he worked from 2000-2002 as Major League Baseball's vice president of on-field operations. Robinson is shown here in a classic Ozzie portrait from 1966 (opposite page), as a young Cincinnati star in 1964 (top left) and in 2003 as Expos manager.

"THE BABE RUTH OF PHOTOGRAPHERS"

THE MASTER
Ozzie Sweet during his heyday as
a 1950s cover photographer.

This book has been in the works for, oh, six decades. It begins, really, in 1947, which happened to be a monumental season for our national pastime. That was the year that Major League Baseball was opening its doors, finally, to African-American ballplayers. Coincidentally, 1947 was the year Ozzie Sweet attended spring training for the first time. *Newsweek* sent the 29-year-old photographer, a rising star in his field, to Arizona to capture Bob Feller on film.

Using his large, boxy, impressive-looking 4 x 5 view camera with tripod, Sweet produced an extreme low-angle view of Feller in his stretch, hands over head, clear blue sky behind him. The resulting portrait landed on *Newsweek*'s June 2, 1947 cover. Who knew that this one photograph would cause a chain-reaction series of events—twists and turns that would push Ozzie Sweet into all kinds of new territory (and innovations) during the decades that followed?

The first twist of fate involved a man named Ed Fitzgerald, editor of *SPORT*—the day's leading publication for sports fans. Sweet's view of Feller stopped Fitzgerald in his tracks. He looked at it, located the cover credit, hunted down Sweet's number, contacted him, and asked if he'd work for *SPORT*.

Fitzgerald's call was well timed. "I had just decided to become a freelancer and to work for a variety of publications," Sweet recalls. Just like that, Ozzie was on board as a regular *SPORT* contributor, although he retained his freelance status. Within a few months, he was taking stunning photographs of the likes of Jackie Robinson (his first subject, fittingly, for *SPORT*).

So valued was Sweet's work that *SPORT* began putting his credits on the cover rather than in the Table of Contents. You can see it there on the September 1949 issue, in the lower-left corner of that wondrously sharp portrait of Joe DiMaggio (Page 18). Inside, *SPORT*'s editors offered this assessment: "We privately think Ozzie Sweet's picture is the greatest portrait of DiMag ever made...."

(Continued on Page 16)

COVER BOY

The name Ozzie Sweet has been synonymous with outstanding photography for almost 60 years. That's Ozzie as a boy in the 1920s (top, right). By the 1950s, when he was shooting all the biggest names in sport, including Ted Williams (right), Sweet was No. 1 in his field. On the opposite page, in a photograph taken in the mid-1960s, Ozzie displays a collage of covers he shot for *SPORT* magazine. He adopted a new look (top) in the 1970s. Ozzie was still going strong in 1999, when he visited the Yankees training camp (above) to shoot Tino Martinez and Paul O'Neill, and in 2003, when he took a moment to pose for our camera (top, left).

Throughout the 1950s and '60s, Sweet seemed to regularly outdo himself, whether he was putting Mickey Mantle or Willie Mays in a powerful, heroic batting stance or taking a sublime portrait of Ted Williams or Sandy Koufax. And he accomplished the bulk of his baseball work—"I'd say around ninety percent of it," Sweet estimates—at spring training on his annual jaunts to Florida or Arizona. He'd plan ahead before his trips and then he'd stay impeccably organized, using his six to eight weeks at training camps to produce dozens and dozens of his high-quality images. *SPORT*'s editors would guide him in terms of the subjects and sometimes cover ideas but, often, Ozzie developed a lot of his own creative concepts. They often involved his patented re-creations of players as they looked in action. Sweet, in fact, has a phrase for them: "simulated action" (see Chapter 2). He'd spend days planning backgrounds, settings, props, and stand-ins, and then he'd bring in a Mantle or a Mays or a Robinson to "act." Today, those vintage photographs give us striking glimpses into baseball's glory days.

After spring training, Sweet had the better part of a year to take on all kinds of other jobs. That freedom allowed him to stick to his plan for variety while also pursuing a related goal: to become a magazine cover specialist. Florida was ideal for a photographer who worked in a variety of topics. In Sweet's case, he'd stay in Florida for several weeks after spring training to do all kinds of photo shoots that required beautiful weather and sunshine. He'd often photograph beautiful women, for example, in set-up beach scenes that often told a story or reflected his sense of humor. He'd primarily use unknowns as his models, conducting his own talent searches with the help of an assistant. He'd sometimes photograph well-known personalities, among them Victoria Principal (Page 26).

By the time Sweet headed north for the summer, he'd have dozens and dozens of cover-quality photographs—and then he'd sell them to a variety of different magazines looking for a fresh, creative cover shot. If you were to visit a newsstand in the 1950s or '60s,

you would have seen multiple magazines bearing Sweet covers; one particular month, he recalls, there were 17 of his covers on display at the same time! Ozzie's photographs graced everything from *Time, Collier's, Look,* and *Argosy* to *TV Guide, Boys' Life, Sports Afield,* and *Field & Stream.* He had cover photographs on *Family Circle, Cosmopolitan,* and *Parents'* as well as *True Romance, Modern Photography,* and *Successful Farming,* among hordes of others.

In fact, if you were to look through Sweet's 1940s, '50s, and '60s archives today, you'd likely have the same reaction I do every time I visit him: *How the hell did he have time to do all that?* And we haven't even touched on his 1970s, '80s, and '90s work, when his photographs continued to turn up on the covers of a variety of publications (*Golf, The Sporting News, Sports Illustrated, Yankee, Young Miss...*), giving him a lifetime total of nearly 1,800 magazine and book cover credits. Nor have we mentioned the series of 18 wildlife books, all in black-and-white, that Sweet filled in the 1970s and '80s. Nor have we touched on the half-dozen or so calendars he's been illustrating every year since the 1940s. Nor have we talked about the untold numbers of creative photography jobs Sweet has produced for advertisers. (Among the latter: more than a dozen eye-popping Colorama images used at Grand Central Station in the 1960s and '70s by Kodak at a size of 60 feet wide and 18 feet high—the largest display of its kind in the world at the time.)

Yes, Sweet has created an enormous body of work, one that continues to grow in the 21st century. But within that body of work, it's his *SPORT* magazine photography that's had the furthest reach—and understandably so. In a truly golden era of sports—the 1950s and '60s—millions of Americans connected with their favorite athletes through the sharpness and warmth and humanness of Sweet's images. *SPORT*'s stable of contributors boasted several other top photographers and photo services as well, but Sweet was the pacesetter, the most innovative, the most daring.

(Continued on Page 19)

NEWS MAKER

Ozzie is best known for his *SPORT* magazine photography, but he also shot for many other major publications. The 1947 *Newsweek* cover of Bob Feller (top, right) catapulted Ozzie to fame. To date, he has shot approximately 1,800 covers, and his cover subjects (right) have included Albert Einstein for

Newsweek, Willie Mays for *Time,* and Mickey Mantle-Roger Maris for *Sports Illustrated*.

Ozzie's arrival on the magazine scene in 1947 coincided with the elimination of the color barrier in baseball. Jackie Robinson (above) was the first African-American major leaguer, followed shortly after by Larry Doby (left).

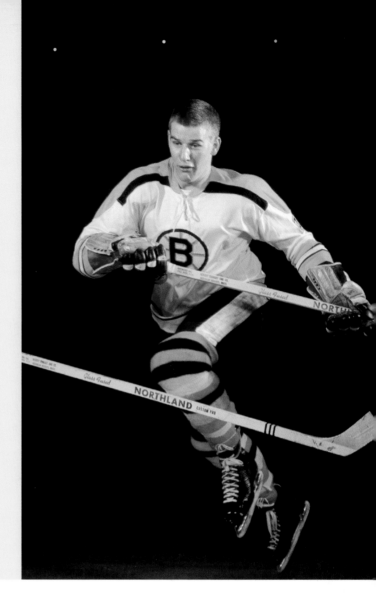

MR. VERSATILITY

When he wasn't shooting baseball covers—including the above examples from *SPORT* that feature (clockwise) Jackie Robinson (1947), Joe DiMaggio (1949), Mickey Mantle-Yogi Berra (1963) and Bobby Thomson (1955)— Ozzie was venturing into other sports. He created a wonderful simulated action portrait of hockey superstar Bobby Orr (top, right) in the late '60s. That's NBA Hall of Famer George Mikan (opposite page, top) in 1950. Ozzie also shot boxing champion Floyd Patterson (opposite page, bottom) in the late '50s, Green Bay star Paul Hornung (right) in 1963, and Mickey Mantle in the mid-'60s.

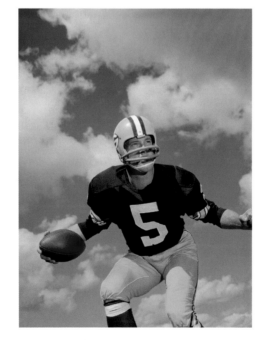

18

BLAST FROM THE PAST

By the 1990s, Ozzie Sweet was doing less photography involving pro athletes and turning his attention more frequently to vintage cars. Then, another twist tugged him back into sports. Baby boomers, as they got into their 30s and 40s and 50s, were growing nostalgic for the treasures and interests from their youth—from toys and baseball cards to music and the glory days of sports. Suddenly, Sweet started enjoying newfound "fame" for work he'd done decades earlier.

Sports Illustrated, in a 1991 "Classic" issue, published an 18-page feature highlighting Sweet's photography. That section helped inspire 1993's *Legends of the Field*, a 268-page book devoted to Sweet classics. And *Legends* led to 1998's *Mickey Mantle: The Yankee Years/The Classic Photography of Ozzie Sweet*. (I had the pleasure of collaborating with Ozzie on the latter, having spent many hours during the previous four years studying his Mantle images. At the time, I was editing a sports memorabilia magazine, *Tuff Stuff*, and on several occasions I used Sweet classics as cover photos.)

Fast-forward to early January 2003. Ozzie Sweet and I are talking on the phone about our plans for the book you're holding. (In fact, we started discussing a baseball-related follow-up to our Mantle book four years earlier, trying on different angles before settling on the most logical: spring training.) During that January 2003 conversation, Ozzie tossed this thought at me, sort of casually: "We should go back to spring training this year and maybe get some photographs of current players...."

Before we knew it, we were headed to Florida, where we hit four camps in four days in March 2003. We returned in 2004 and went back again in 2005 after *Sports Illustrated* gave Ozzie an assignment.

Like so many others who remember *SPORT* magazine, I've been a fan of Sweet's work since I was a baseball-card-carrying kid of the 1960s. I was drawn to his "alive" portraits of baseball's best players along with the stars of football, basketball, hockey, boxing, golf, and even bowling. His portraits of such

superstars as Johnny Unitas, Paul Hornung, Jim Brown, George Mikan, Oscar Robertson, Bobby Orr, Bobby Hull, Floyd Patterson, Rocky Marciano, Jack Nicklaus, and countless others remain emblazoned on the minds of a generation or two.

Within the universe of *SPORT* readers were countless future photographers, impressionable youngsters who took notice of those high-impact photographs and found their own career goals within. As a result, Sweet encountered a surprising outpouring of affection in Florida in 2003, '04 and '05 from today's best lensmen.

At every camp we visited, I met working photographers who were surprised, amazed, even "knocked out," as one said, to see Ozzie Sweet at spring training, doing baseball again at age 84 (in 2003) and 85 (in 2004). His peers—I might better call them his disciples—wanted to meet Ozzie, talk business, ask him how he got those shots back in the day. Almost every one of them asked, "Have you gone digital, Ozzie?" (No, he hasn't. He still uses 2 1/4-inch transparencies with his Hasselblad, which he calls "the Rolls Royce of cameras.") A number of photographers asked for some type of Ozzie memento—an autograph, a business card, a photograph with him. One of them even asked Ozzie, sort of in an embarrassed tone, if he could load his camera for him. (Imagine being a professional photographer today and telling your colleagues, "I loaded Ozzie Sweet's camera!")

Our first stop in 2003 set the tone. At the Houston Astros' facility in Kissimmee, Fla., I struck up a conversation with Rich Pilling, director of photography at Major League Baseball, and mentioned that I was in camp with Ozzie Sweet. "Ozzie Sweet's here?" an excited Pilling asked. "Are you serious?" Moments later, Pilling was telling Sweet, "Ozzie, you're the reason I got into photography. I used to study your photographs for hours."

Chuck Solomon, a top *Sports Illustrated* photographer, also paid homage to Sweet. In 2004, at the Devil Rays' camp in

(Continued on Page 22)

GALLERY OF STARS
Ozzie assembled this "gallery"
of his personal favorite
photographs while living in New
Hampshire in the late 1990s.

St. Petersburg, Solomon sat down and talked about Sweet's influence, calling him "the Babe Ruth of photographers."

"Ozzie helped set the standard for what we do as sports photographers," Solomon says. "If you were to have a sports photographers' hall of fame, Ozzie would be right up near the top—one of the first two or three."

For Solomon, multiple attributes make Sweet's work special. "Ozzie's style was very direct, without any affectation," he says. "As photographs, they're technically excellent. And there was no attitude in Ozzie's photographs...."

"People look at a photograph like his Clemente [holding his cap over his heart, Page 24], and they think it's pretty straightforward, pretty easy to do," Solomon adds. "But I know what it takes to make a photograph like that. You don't have an hour to do things like that, yet Ozzie's photographs are always right on."

Victor Baldizon, a noted freelancer who photographs baseball and basketball for such publications as *ESPN: The Magazine* and *Sports Illustrated*, took time out at Vero Beach in 2004 to talk about the seamlessness of Sweet's work.

"It's the simplicity of his photographs" that Baldizon finds especially inspiring. "Most photographers complicate things—they try to do this, try to do that, try to get intriguing lighting. What I like most [about Sweet's work] was the simplicity. And I like the fact that he used medium-format or large-format [transparencies] for most of his portraits. That was my thing. I wanted to shoot just like he did. Of course, you can't just duplicate what he does, because he's the master.

"If you talk to the big guys of the time [the 1960s and '70s], the Neil Leifers or the Walter Ioosses, all of these people owe something to Ozzie, in some way," Baldizon adds. "If you look at today's Walter Iooss work, he was so influenced by Ozzie."

Walter Iooss Jr.—himself an icon among photographers—is to *Sports Illustrated* what Ozzie Sweet was to *SPORT*. Iooss' career started in the early 1960s, and he counts Sweet among the photographers "who had an impact on me, because they were who I

wanted to be," he says.

Iooss would become a leading action and portrait photographer whose vast credits include some 300 covers for *Sports Illustrated*; his work has also filled a number of books, including *Classic Baseball/The Photography of Walter Iooss.* But back in his formative teenage years of the 1950s, Iooss was one of legions of *SPORT* readers touched by Sweet's photographs.

"Ozzie's work was always bright, with those colorful backgrounds," Iooss says. "I was almost too young to understand lighting technique; the vibrancy of his color really is what I remember. He was the very first colorist."

Just as important to Iooss was the caliber of Sweet's subjects. "He always got the guys who were heroes to me," he says. "I remember his Mantle [portraits] as much anything. Mickey was my hero as a kid, and Ozzie had the chance to photograph him like no one else."

Sweet's Mantle, Iooss says, typifies the photographer's work: "Tight, strong portraiture. Color. In your face."

Yet "the one I remember most," Iooss says, "is the black-and-white fishing-trip photograph. That may be his greatest photograph. It was a beautiful 'off' moment. It reminds me of *Ocean's 11*; these guys [Mantle, Billy Martin, Whitey Ford, and Bob Grim] were hell-raisers. They were like the Rat Pack—Sinatra, Martin, Lewis, and Davis."

Iooss is talking about an image from a landmark series taken during a deep-sea fishing excursion that Sweet arranged in 1956. Spring training was just ending; as the Yankees broke camp in St. Petersburg, Sweet invited Mantle, Martin, Ford, and Grim to go fishing. The resulting photographs included more than a dozen black-and-white images. There was also a lone color image from the fishing trip, and that one stands as perhaps Sweet's most celebrated photograph.

"There's something so positive about it," Baldizon says. "It has beautiful energy: a group of guys sitting back, having a Coke on an afternoon fishing trip. See how the subjects are absent from the camera? They don't feel its

(Continued on Page 25)

GONE FISHING

Ozzie excelled at building close working relationships with athletes, which led to him joining a group of Yankees on a 1956 Florida fishing trip. A master of candid shots, he created this classic (from left to right) of Mickey Mantle, Bob Grim, Billy Martin and Whitey Ford.

"That may be his greatest photograph. It was a beautiful 'off' moment."

"His work stood out in much the same
way that Norman Rockwell art does."

STAR POWER

Ozzie's 1949 portrait of Joe DiMaggio (top, left) is considered a classic, as is his 1970 profile of Roberto Clemente (left). Sandy Koufax, photographed here in 1970 (above), always had time, and a smile, for Ozzie. In 1950, Ozzie got Ralph Kiner to pose amid a sea of autograph hounds.

presence. This, for me, is perhaps the most beautiful moment I've seen. It'll go right there with the greatest pictures ever."

And it wouldn't have happened without the access to athletes that became a Sweet trademark. "To be accepted, to even be there, you have to be admired [by the athletes]," Baldizon points out. "You don't talk your way into that type of situation."

At an early age, Sweet understood that it's essential to build relationships with your subjects. Ballplayers, Baldizon says, "have to know that you're there to build something positive. This is not a paparazzi business, where you go around trying to build sensation. You either create beauty or you don't create."

Richard Johnson, curator of the New England Sports Museum in Boston, also appreciates the mutual respect between Sweet and his subjects.

"Ozzie Sweet was, in photography, what his subjects were in their own endeavors," Johnson says. "His reputation preceded him. It was a privilege for his subjects to be photographed by him. He was a hale fellow, well-met, a throwback to photographers of old. The earliest photographers had to be characters—they had to be very personable to engage their subjects to sit for them.

"Photographers today, because of technology and the nature of sports and commerce, have to be snipers almost, whereas Ozzie was and is a person who developed relationships beyond the opening and closing of a shutter," Johnson says. "If the old saying is true that a picture is worth a thousand words, there must have been a thousand words spoken before Ozzie took his photographs."

Neil Leifer, another luminary among photographers, puts it like this: "Athletes must have just loved Ozzie. You couldn't beat the cooperation he got; it was amazing to me. He's something of a legend in our business."

Leifer began his career in 1960 while still in his teens. He quickly became a top photographer for *Sports Illustrated* as well as *Time, Life, Look, Newsweek, Saturday Evening Post*, and countless others. "I grew up looking at *SPORT* magazine," Leifer says, "and Ozzie

was one of my favorite photographers. In the mid-1950s, when I began paying attention to photo credits, Ozzie's pictures stood out. In fact, you didn't even need to see his name, because his work stood out in much the same way that Norman Rockwell's art does. Ozzie had a style that he mastered, and he did it perfectly. He was able to make an art form where one didn't exist. He took pictures I remember and, to this day, I love."

THE MAKING OF A PHOTOGRAPHER

To gain an understanding of what makes Sweet special, your best bet is to turn back the clock and consider the man's natural talents, characteristics, and experiences. When you know what went into the making of this photographer—the creative spirit; his roles as an actor; his interest in directing; a military stint that fed him discipline, planning and organization—it all makes sense.

He was born in Stamford, Conn., on Sept. 10, 1918—"just two weeks after my uncle Oscar Henry Cowan had been killed in France" at the end of World War I, he says. "At the time I was born, my mother didn't know about her brother; they didn't want anything to go wrong [with her pregnancy], although my father knew." His mother already had it in her mind, however, to use her brother's name if the baby was a boy. And so he was named Oscar, with Cowan as his middle name.

When young Ozzie was three years old, the Sweets moved to the Adirondacks, to a small town, New Russia, N.Y., located 35 miles from Lake Placid.

Early on, he went by Oscar Sweet, but "that was kind of a sissy name," he says, laughing. "I took a lot teasing, and had to use my dukes at times." In high school, "Oscar" became "Ozzie." By then, he was already showing signs of his trademark resilience. He was an enterprising youngster who, in his pre-teen years, made money by selling flowers to his neighbors. Later he earned money as a caddy. After high school, he felt the tug of the west and went away to college at the Art Center in Los Angeles.

In the late 1930s, Sweet found his way into

several movies, including *Hopalong Cassidy* and John Wayne films. His big break came via an attention-getting stunt: He rented two parking spots across the street from Paramount Studio, where famed director Cecil B. DeMille was making *Reap the Wild Wind*, starring Wayne. Sweet camped out under a hand-made sign that read, "Part in 'Reap the Wild Wind' or Bust." After local newspapers featured him in their Hollywood columns, he got a support role in the film.

Around the same time, he was developing an interest in photography. "I worked as an apprentice for a well-known photographer, Louis Kramer, at Long Beach, California," he recalls.

World War II derailed Sweet's acting career, but not his interest in photography. After being drafted, he completed basic training and then settled in with the Signal Corp at Camp Callan, near San Diego. Later, he was commissioned as a 2nd lieutenant in the U.S. Air Force. He spent five years in the service, using the time to hone his skills as a photographer.

While in the service, Sweet began submitting his photographs to national publications, and he found quick success. Between fall 1942 and summer 1943, he notched eight cover credits with seven different magazines, including *Newsweek*. He also drew the attention of *Popular Photography*, which profiled him in a feature story called "Cover Conscious." Photographer Sweet, according to the story, "has netted himself a handsome amount of cash while operating minus a studio or list of professional models, and usually with barely enough capital to acquire the film."

After finishing his military duty, Sweet got hired as a staff photographer by *Newsweek*. During the mid-1940s, he would produce dozens of cover photos, including memorable images of Ingrid Bergman, Jimmy Durante, James Mason—and Bob "Rapid Robert" Feller. Of course, on that warm March morning in 1947, as he looked up at Feller through his lens, not even Ozzie Sweet could have envisioned where this particular photograph might lead him.

Nor could he have predicted that 58 years later, he'd be looking through his camera at the young ballplayers of a new century.

A month or so before the Feller shoot, Sweet photographed another fairly famous figure: Albert Einstein. They had some laughs together, the genius and the young photographer. Sweet teased Einstein, he remembers, by saying that he noticed the way the backs of his Oxford-style shoes were flattened (easier to slip on and off)—and that it gave him "a certain dash." "He really cracked up," Sweet says. "He was such a jolly fellow."

During that memorable session, some of Einstein's philosophies apparently seeped into Sweet's soul, because Ozzie has practiced them for his entire career:

"We have to do the best we can.
This is our sacred human responsibility."

"Life is like riding a bicycle.
To keep your balance you must keep moving."

"...Do not grow old no matter how long [you] live."

VICTORIA'S SECRET

At the end of spring training each spring, Ozzie often remained behind in Florida on photo shoots that required bright sunshine, perfect weather and beautiful women. In addition to the photos on this page, you'll notice examples of these often 'offbeat' creations—many of which demonstrate Ozzie's keen sense of humor—displayed on several of the chapter fronts of this book. For the most part, Ozzie used unknown models, but occasionally he happened upon a rising star, such as Victoria Principal (opposite page).

THE BOYS OF SPRING

CHAPTER ONE

GETTING LOOSE

"I see spring training as one of baseball's most appealing traditions. The teams come in with high hopes, and they spend several weeks in a positive frame of mind. The players work on their games without the pressure of a pennant race, so the atmosphere feels calm, almost carefree."

OZZIE

Florida can provide a swingin'-good time for vacationers, as Ozzie illustrated with this early-1960s photograph, created for a travel agency.

Baseball's long, illustrious history is filled with unforgettable moments—some that we recall simply from a statistic (61, for example), others from the mere mention of a name (Bucky Dent), still others from a phrase ("The Shot Heard 'Round the World"). Usually, such moments came amidst high drama, whether it was a classic pitcher-hitter duel (remember the tension of the Mariano Rivera-Luis Gonzalez 9th-inning showdown in the 2001 World Series?) or a bounding ball that slipped through an infielder's legs to lose a World Series game (hello, Bill Buckner). The list could fill volumes and volumes of books—and indeed has.

Then there's the polar opposite of such moments: spring training baseball.

Ah, springtime in Florida and Arizona. Forget Disney World, alligator parks, the beach, and NASCAR. Never mind golf vacations, Old West attractions, and scenic desert landscapes. February and March mean spring training, when Major League Baseball's full complement of teams—18 in Florida, 12 in Arizona—begin their hunt for the ring. This is the time of year when the forecast for every ballclub is sunny, when optimism runs rampant from the front office down to the youngest rookie. Every team has a shot at the title. Every player has a chance to make the team.

But before the first pitch of pre-season baseball, before the first swing of a Hillerich & Bradsby, before the first bouncer up the middle, players go through routines and regimens that are time-tested and traditional. They stretch. They play catch. They long-toss. They run. They sprint. They lift. They work their bodies hard in preparing for the demands of a long season.

Of course, today's players rarely get out of shape. Years ago, the off-season meant winter jobs—as in, real work—for the average big leaguer. Today, they're hardly necessary: The average salary skyrocketed from $25,000 in 1969 to $513,000 in 1989 to $2.5 million in 2004. Instead of working in a supermarket during the off-season (as Roger Maris did in

1958), today's players simply work out, so most of them come to camp practically in playing condition.

Even so, those regimens of spring training remain. And with them come hordes of media representing magazines, newspapers, book publishers, Internet sites, and radio and TV stations. There are writers and editors, reporters and statisticians, announcers and analysts, videographers and soundmen—and, of course, photographers. They're looking for the spectacular, but in the relaxed air of spring training, they're more likely to see the mundane: players getting loose or shagging flies.

Now, watching ballplayers run through drills may not be the most riveting view for photographers, but it's always been a welcome sight for Ozzie Sweet.

"I see spring training as one of baseball's most appealing traditions," he says. "The teams come in with high hopes, and they spend several weeks in a positive frame of mind. The players work on their games without the pressure of a pennant race, so the atmosphere feels calm, almost carefree."

With that in mind, Sweet has been enjoying, observing, and photographing the landscape of spring training for decades, dating back to his first baseball assignment in 1947 for *Newsweek*. In the years that followed, it was during spring training that Sweet executed his impossibly detailed portraits and elaborately staged "simulated action" photographs.

At the same time, he made a point of capturing spring rituals—the calisthenics, the behind-the-scenes conditioning, the batting practice. He'd seek out angles and views that no one else looks for. He'd find striking forms, odd arrangements of equipment, interesting faces. And always he'd watch for those inevitable moments of tomfoolery and sheer fun.

Fun in the sun was a theme that permeated all of Ozzie's work in Florida. In this tourism bureau photograph he recreated an idyllic 1960s beach scene.

FUN IN THE SUN

As we said, Ozzie had an eye for tomfoolery. We give you Exhibit A—his wide-angle, wonderfully spontaneous view of the 1976 Boston Red Sox. Sweet happened to capture the Red Sox as they charged out of their clubhouse, ready to go to battle after the heartbreak of the 1975 World Series, when not even the dramatic 12th-inning home run Carlton Fisk hit to win Game 6 could keep the Cincinnati Reds from winning a title.

If the Red Sox were suffering any carryover depression on that day in Winter Haven, Fla., in 1976, it isn't evident in this unguarded photograph.

"This one is so spring training," Ozzie says. "It's got trees, the guys having fun, a camera in the background. And I like the way the Red Sox are running out onto the field—it's like stepping out on a stage."

Up front is steady Cecil Cooper, calm as the Florida sky (in the middle of the photograph, carrying his bat). To his left is an intense Fred Lynn appearing to let out a primal scream. Running a few steps directly behind Cooper is Carl Yastrzemski, looking very much like a captain with that puffed-chest jog. And notice Rick Burleson—obviously aware of Sweet's camera—flashing "bunny ears" behind the head of an unsuspecting Luis Tiant.

Also in the picture are pitchers Don Aase (to Yaz's right) and Jim Willoughby (wearing the blue jacket). And outfielder Bernie Carbo is in there (behind and to the left of Lynn), as are second basemen Doug Griffin and Denny Doyle (far right).

This is the type of image that can't be set up or orchestrated. It's just good luck. As always, Ozzie was in the right place at the right time.

BOYS OF BOSTON

Sweet's visit to the Red Sox camp in 1976 produced a variety of images presented here for the first time. Several feature Fred Lynn, who was attracting all kinds of attention after his spectacular Rookie-of-the-Year season in 1975, when he hit .331 with 21 homers, and 105 RBI. You can see him below, for example, as he limbers up before fielding drills.

"I spent a whole day following him around and banged away," recalls Ozzie. "I got grabs as well as carefully planned close-ups. And Fred was great—a nice and easygoing guy."

Ozzie also captured many of Lynn's teammates. At left, pitcher Dick Pole is helping a teammate stretch (notice Carl Yastrzemski, No. 8, in the background). On the opposite page, in a "tools of the trade" study, Sweet frames a Red Sox player's mitt with the gloves of Doug Griffin (left) and Yastrzemski (right).

"I spent a whole day following him around and banged away."

POINTS OF VIEW

Ozzie loved to wander the field in search of the rare angle to take a photograph. He was delighted to happen upon this 'through the wickets' perspective (left) of an upside-down Fred Lynn. Other sights and scenes from the Red Sox camp include these unique batting-cage views.

In the bottom photograph, shortstop Rick Burleson, No. 7, takes his cuts in the cage while a trio of hopefuls looks on. That's first baseman Jack Baker wearing No. 41, which he inherited when Dick Drago was traded to the Angels a couple of weeks earlier. Wearing No. 4 is rookie Clell Lavern Hobson, better known as Butch. At the time of this photograph, Hobson had barely tasted the big leagues (four at-bats in 1975). He would hit only .234 in 1976, but he followed that season with a .265, 30-homer season in 1977. As for No. 25, that's none other than Tony Conigliaro. Wait a minute—Tony Conigliaro? Didn't he retire in mid-1975? He did, but he returned to spring training in 1976 to check in on his friends, while suiting up to take some swings.

Conigliaro also appears in the top photograph, taking his cuts in the cage while Denny Doyle, wearing No. 5 in his first spring training with the Red Sox, waits on deck. Also pictured in the top photograph: backup catcher Tim Blackwell, No. 39 (he was sold to the Phillies within weeks of this photo), coach Eddie Popowski, No. 36, and Hobson (No. 4).

TOOLS OF THE TRADE

One of Ozzie's prized possessions is his Hasselblad camera. Today, when more and more photographers are carrying digital equipment, Ozzie's Hasselblad is a throwback to a different era. It was even a curiosity in 1976, when Ozzie allowed Fred Lynn (right) to try it on for size. The payback is seen above, as Ozzie posed Lynn, using teammate Doug Griffin's bat, in the classic slugger's stance.

In the photo at right, Red Sox catcher Carlton Fisk leads off third base, with Rico Petrocelli at the plate, in a 1976 Red Sox/Astros spring training game.

VERO BEACH

Ozzie Sweet's favorite spring training site is Vero Beach, Fla., where the Dodgers train. The ballpark there is as charming as any you'll find, thanks to such unique stylings as the open-air dugouts. "The players can get a little hot sitting there for entire games in the sun, with no shade, but the fans love it," Sweet says. "The ones in the front rows behind the dugouts can actually reach out and touch the players."

You'll see several photographs taken at Vero Beach in this book. On this page is a candid of Dodger second baseman Davey Lopes finding relief (left) from the spring heat inside a towel in March 1978. Lopes was hot in a lot of ways around that time: He hit .283 with 43 stolen bases in 1977, and, in 1978, .278 with 45 steals in helping L.A. win the NL pennant. In a losing cause in the 1978 World Series, Lopes was spectacular, batting .308 with three homers, seven RBI, and two steals against the New York Yankees.

Sweet also caught Lopes lying on the spring grass (below), blowing a bubble, before a 1978 spring training game. Relaxing are outfielder Rick Monday (No. 16); rookie Rick Sutcliffe (No. 48); and catcher Steve Yeager (wearing a helmet). In the center of things is coach Jim Gilliam (No. 19), who died of a stroke later in the year—on Oct. 8, 1978, just two days before Los Angeles was to face the Yankees in the World Series. Gilliam, a lifelong Dodger, played from 1953 through 1966. He spent the last two years of his career as a player-coach and became a full-time member of the Dodgers' coaching staff up until the time of his death.

"The players can get a little hot sitting there for entire games in the sun, with no shade, but the fans love it."

PLAYFUL PEDRO

Gilliam's last season coincided with the first major league appearance of Pedro Guerrero, a slugger who experienced short stints with the Dodgers in 1978, '79, and '80 before winning a full-time job in 1981, when he batted .300 in a strike-interrupted season. The following spring, 1982, Sweet captured Guerrero playing the drums during a pre-game event and then goofing on a female photographer. Guerrero stayed in a good mood throughout the 1982 season, batting .304 with 32 home runs and 100 RBI. He followed with remarkably similar numbers in 1983: .298, 32 HRs, and 103 RBI. He finished his career in 1992 with the Cardinals with a lifetime .300 average and 215 home runs.

REMARKABLE REGGIE

The Dodgers and Yankees met in the World Series in 1977, '78, and '81, with the Yankees prevailing in the first two encounters and the Dodgers coming back to win in '81. Among the gallery of stars that kept the Yankees in contention was Reginald Martinez Jackson, the enigmatic outfielder known as much for his brashness as his power at the plate. This is the man who once said, "After Jackie Robinson, the most important black in baseball history is Reggie Jackson; I really mean that." A teammate of Jackson in his Oakland A's days, pitcher Darold Knowles,

"When you unwrap a 'Reggie!' bar, it tells you how good it is."

once said, "There isn't enough mustard in the whole world to cover that hot dog." And early in his career, Jackson speculated that if he ever played for the Yankees, "they'd name a candy bar after me." As it turned out, "they" (Standard Brands, a Manhattan-based company) did, prompting another teammate, Jim "Catfish" Hunter, to quip, "When you unwrap a 'Reggie!' bar, it tells you how good it is."

With a three-homer performance in Game 6 of the 1977 World Series, Jackson cemented his nickname: "Mr. October." The following spring, Sweet visited the Yankees' camp and grabbed a revealing close-up of Jackson (below). Sweet remembers the aura surrounding the man: "He had a real flair, even at spring training," Sweet says. "People kept their eyes on him. Just

from his general manner, you could tell he was more of a showman—not a show-off, but a showman. He was maybe more conscious of being watched, of being popular, than other players."

Two years later, in 1981, Sweet photographed Jackson again at spring training (at left), this time kibitzing with pitching instructor Whitey Ford. (The black armbands worn by the Yankees that year were in honor of Elston Howard, who died in December 1980.) For Jackson, the 1981 season, his last with the Yankees, would be forgettable. By now 35, he hit only .237 with 15 home runs in 334 at-bats.

POTENT PIRATES

Does anyone at spring training seem to glow more than a Rookie of the Year from the previous season? Not likely, as this Ozzie shot of Jason Bay illustrates. Sweet photographed Bay in 2005 at charming old McKechnie Field in Bradenton, where the NL's top 2004 rookie was preparing to take batting practice. Note the detail and vivid colors in this classic-style portrait.

Pittsburgh acquired Bay and Oliver Perez from the Padres in August 2003 for All-Star outfielder Brian Giles. The trade was unpopular in the Steel City at the time, but the new Pirates paid instant dividends. In 2004, Bay—a 6-foot-2, 205-pounder from Canada—hit .282 with 26 homers. As for Perez, the third-year lefty pitcher went 12-10 with a 2.98 ERA and 239 strikeouts in 196 innings.

A full 25 years earlier, Ozzie was in Bradenton photographing the 1980 Pirates, including bespectacled Kent Tekulve (below). The angular (6-foot-4, 180 pounds) right-hander had a delivery that could confound hitters; it was all arms and legs. Tekulve saved 184 games and posted a 2.85 ERA in his 16-year career, but he was at his best in 1979, saving 31 games and winning 10 others while posting a 2.75 ERA. In the Pirates' seven-game World Series win over the Orioles, Tekulve pitched in five games, saved three, and struck out 10 batters in 9.3 innings.

Sweet's photograph of Tekulve finds him fraternizing with a pair of role players on the St. Louis Cardinals: Mike Phillips and Jim Lentine.

"Baseball can bring out the kid in anyone."

BUBBLE-HEAD BOYS

Baseball and bubblegum have had a tight relationship for years, but which came first? Our national pastime actually predates bubblegum by a good half-century; Walter Diemer invented modern bubblegum, calling it Double Bubble, in 1928. (Years earlier, in 1906, Henry Fleer's brother Frank created a form of the sweet confection called Blibber-Blabber, but it never sold well—too sticky.) In the 1930s, the first baseball card packs to include gum began landing on store shelves. And during the baseball card's blowout years, the 1950s and '60s, when Topps ruled the marketplace, gum was a mainstay in card packs—hence the phrase "bubblegum cards."

In 1975, Major League Baseball sponsored the Bazooka/Joe Garagiola Bubble-Blowing contest for players. The winner: Kurt Bevacqua, who played for the Milwaukee Brewers at the time. A few years later, in the early 1980s, Ozzie Sweet happened to catch Rick Rhoden, a one-time teammate of Bevacqua's, practicing his own bubble-blowing skills (top, left). That photograph reminds us that "baseball can bring out the kid in anyone," as Sweet says. By the mid-1990s, Topps stopped putting gum in packs of cards, in part because it tended to stain the cardboard. Yet bubblegum and baseball still go together. Twenty-four years after shooting Rhoden, Sweet spotted the Mets' Jae Seo blowing bubbles and asked him to hold one. Seo delivered only a so-so result under pressure—but it was good enough to make the cut.

MEDIA MADNESS

As a member of the media, Ozzie Sweet appreciates the efforts of his peers—the challenges they face, the creativity they show, and their role in bringing the national pastime to fans. As such, he tends to notice unique "photo ops" involving the working press. An example: Sweet captures a videographer creeping up on backup Dodger catcher Dave Sax (below) in the early 1980s. Sax is talking to a teammate (hidden from view) while he loosens up, and several Dodgers stars surround them: Bob Welch, Dusty Baker, Burt Hooton, and Ron Cey. We also get a Sweet view of digital camera equipment, 21st-century style (bottom, right). That's Rich Pilling, director of photography for Major League

Baseball, aiming his lens at a Houston Astros player in Kissimmee, Fla., in 2003. Pilling says as a young photographer he was inspired by Sweet.

At right are two more examples of the media at work, both taken in the 1980s. In one, a videographer decked out in rain gear weathers a Florida storm. In the other, a cameraman waits out a period of inactivity, catching some rays during his downtime.

One significant difference in the baseball media, Sweet has noticed over the years, is the emergence of females on the job. "In the 1940s and '50s," he says, "there were very few women reporters, photographers, announcers. These were male-dominated jobs, and it took a while for

things to change." On the opposite page we see evidence of that change: female reporters interviewing Denny McLain of the Senators in 1971 and Yogi Berra, as a Yankees coach, in 1981. The latter is a "fly-on-the-wall" grab by Sweet, who has always enjoyed focusing on Berra, dating back to the 1940s and '50s. The McLain photo, Sweet admits, features just a bit of prompting. "McLain actually did get interviewed by the [unidentified] television reporter in the photograph," he says. "But after they finished, I asked them to hold their poses, and I moved them closer together for better composition. Doesn't Denny look like he's really enjoying the interview?"

"Doesn't Denny look like he's really enjoying the interview?"

RALPH HOUK AND COMPANY

Spring training offers a chance for old buddies to catch up, and for former Yankee manager Ralph Houk, there was never a shortage of old friends—players, peers, opponents—to track down. The proof is to be seen on these pages: a group of photographs in which Ozzie Sweet—not necessarily focusing on Houk—caught him exchanging war stories with old pals.

Starting on the opposite page, we see Houk (top) in the early 1980s as Boston's manager, getting advice from instructor Ted Williams. Houk would manage the Red Sox from 1981 through 1984, posting a record of 312-282. Below them, Houk is giving an interview. At bottom, Houk, a former Detroit Tigers manager, talks things over with Yankee coach Yogi Berra in 1978. At the time, Houk was starting the last of five challenging seasons as the Tigers' skipper. (Houk's combined record with the Tigers was 363-443.)

On this page, Houk sits back with Mickey Mantle (top), whom he managed during his reign as the Yankees' skipper (1961 through '73; his record: 944-806 with two championships). Mantle often traveled to Florida after his 1969 retirement to serve as a spring training instructor for the Yankees. Left, we see Houk having a laugh with Billy Martin before a 1978 spring training game.

"THE OL' PERFESSOR"

Ralph Houk had a great role model when it came to media relations: Casey Stengel. On these pages are two classic Sweet portraits of "The Ol' Perfessor." The first, at right, was taken before the 1949 season—Stengel's first as the Yankees' manager. There's never been a sharper, more revealing photograph of Stengel—unless it's the portrait on the opposite page, taken by Sweet 15 years (and seven World Championships) later, in 1964, when Casey was managing the New York Mets.

"When I first photographed him, Casey was an older manager and I was a young fella. He was all business during our sessions, but very cooperative too—he'd look right smack into the lens," said Ozzie.

Spring training is usually a time of high hopes and great expectations, but not even Stengel could have been optimistic when he took over the expansion Mets in 1962. These were not the Yankees, after all. Stengel took his lumps in '62, struggling to eke out 40 wins (against 120 losses) from his new team. He improved by 11 wins in 1963 (51-111) and two more in 1964 (53-109). But 95 games into the 1965 season, with the Mets still stumbling (31-64), the team's front office replaced Stengel with Wes Westrum, who found out the job was no picnic, posting a 19-48 record. Stengel's "Amazin' Mets" experience hardly tarnished his reputation: He was inducted into the Hall of Fame in 1966.

"He was all business during our sessions, but very cooperative too—he'd look right smack into the lens."

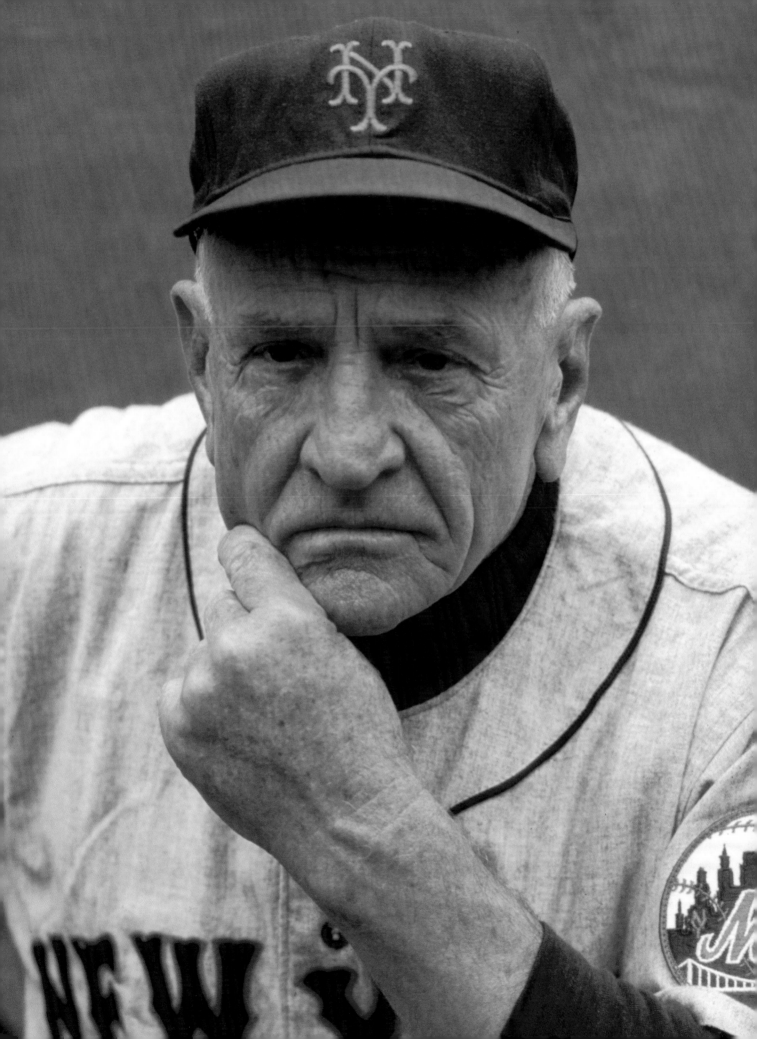

TALKATIVE TOMMY

Vero Beach was the place to be in the early 1980s. Guys like manager Tommy Lasorda and first baseman Steve Garvey of the Dodgers made it a fun camp, as Ozzie fondly recalls. He made a habit of photographing the pair, with several highlights showing up on these two pages. In one pairing of candids (opposite page), Lasorda, who always had something to say, is granting an interview to a TV reporter—only to undergo some good-natured ribbing by Garvey, who's pretending to roll film at Lasorda's face.

Sweet was a master of the closeup. Here he comes in tight on both Lasorda and Garvey to create revealing portraits that emphasize their unmistakable profiles.

Lasorda, by the time these photographs were taken, had established himself as a charismatic, effective leader. He had big shoes to fill—he replaced Walter Alston in 1976 after Alston had logged 23 seasons, 2,040 wins, and four championships. Lasorda was up to the task, managing 21 years and winning 1,599 games and three championships.

Garvey played for the Dodgers from late 1969 through '82 before signing with the San Diego Padres, where he put in five years. He retired in 1987 with 272 home runs, 2,599 hits, and a .294 average, four Gold Gloves at first base, and an MVP award (1974).

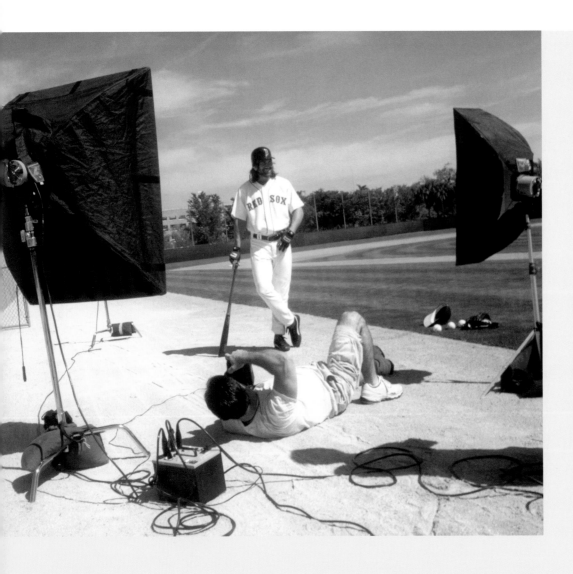

A STAR IS BORN

At Fort Myers in 2005, Ozzie photographed Johnny Damon, leadoff hitter and longhaired style-setter for the 2004 champion Red Sox. Above, he captured Damon signing for fans.

Damon has said he's interested in acting after baseball. Good call, says Sweet: "He has nice features and a great personality and attitude. Everything about him should spell success as an actor." For now, Damon gets plenty of looks from still cameras. At left, he strikes a pose for Tom DiPace, a top photographer and a longtime fan of Sweet's. DiPace's elaborate outdoor studio, Ozzie says, reminds him of his own set-ups in the 1950s and '60s, with one major difference: He used "great big blue flashbulbs, which matched the color of the sky," Sweet says, "and they had to be changed after every shot."

PEN PALS

Fans have long known that spring training is a gold mine for autograph collecting. Because of the casual, generally low-pressure atmosphere, players are more likely to be "in the mood." As such, Ozzie has always enjoyed photographing players signing for fans. His archives include plenty of candid shots, many of which are reproduced on the pages that follow. But Ozzie also liked to create his own autograph scenes. He enjoyed finding young, enthusiastic fans that he could pose with photogenic ballplayers.

On this page, Ozzie set up this Norman Rockwell-like shot with a player he believes is a young Cleon Jones. The shot would have been taken in 1965, when Jones wore No. 34 (he later switched to No. 21). The other photo shows Dodgers first baseman Steve Garvey signing for admiring fans in the early 1980s. This one was no set-up: Garvey was a favorite at Vero Beach and, more often than not, was happy to oblige the fans.

DODGER GREATS

One of Ozzie's favorite autograph shots is this photo of Sandy Koufax (left) signing for a female fan. This one succeeds because Koufax's reaction is so honest. "He's looking at her with an admiring eye, almost flirting, like he really appreciates her," Sweet says. The woman with Koufax is a fan, not a model, Sweet says. In fact, Ozzie often surveyed the stands in spring training in search of the right faces to feature in these types of photographs. That led him to set up this 1950s shot (below) in which Pee Wee Reese is posing amid several female admirers.

A RARE SMILE

Complementing the outstanding Koufax image is a real find: a wonderful look at Roger Maris from 1962 (right). The smile is genuine, albeit rare: Maris was known to avoid the media, yet he obviously considered Sweet an ally. He may also have still been riding the high of his 61-homer season from the previous season.

"He's looking at her with an admiring eye, almost flirting, like he really appreciates her."

*"I asked Mickey to talk to them to get their attention,
and he helped me—he was the one who got those genuine,
happy expressions from the kids."*

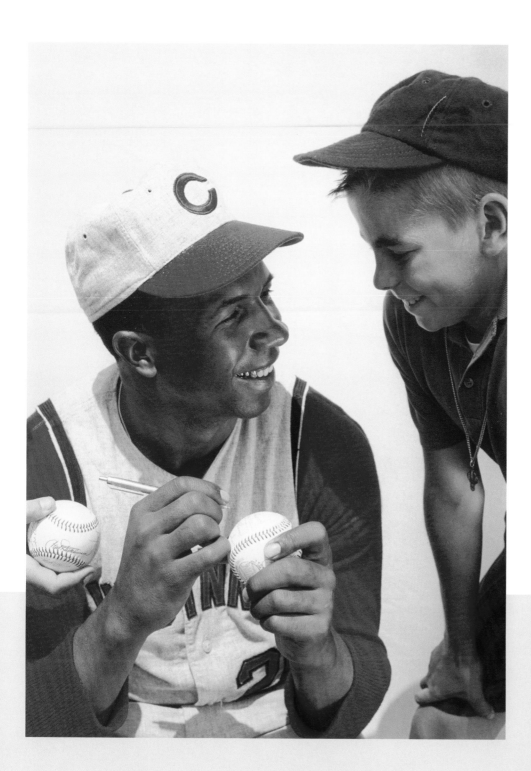

HERO WORSHIP

Often, baseball-crazy boys fit the bill as Ozzie models, as Sweet found in directing these shoots involving Mickey Mantle and Frank Robinson. These images epitomize Sweet's magic: enthusiastic, smiling fans, cooperative heroes, crystal-clear focus, and bright colors.

Ozzie set up the shot with Mantle (far left) in 1962. "When I photographed these young boys getting their hero's autograph, I wanted them to be really, really interested in Mickey and to forget the camera was there. So I asked Mickey to talk to them to get their attention, and he helped me—he was the one who got those genuine, happy expressions from the kids."

By 1964 Frank Robinson was an established star, putting him clearly in Ozzie's sights. The detail in the photograph here is spectacular; note the autographs of Fred Hutchinson (Reds manager) and Ted Davidson (rookie pitcher) on one of the balls offered to Robinson.

Then there's Pete Rose, who looks just a little stoic in this "simulated autograph" photo (right). Ozzie returned to his tried-and-true formula in 1970 with Rose. As it turns out, this image was a sign of things to come: Rose would become a regular on the autograph show circuit, appearing frequently at card shows and conventions in the 1990s and early 2000s. His competitive spirit shows up even in this arena: "He was the fastest signer I've ever seen," recalls Matt Smith, a Richmond, Va., show promoter for several years in the 1990s. "He's a machine."

Also shown here making the fans happy are Luis Tiant, 1979 (below), and Rusty Staub, 1976.

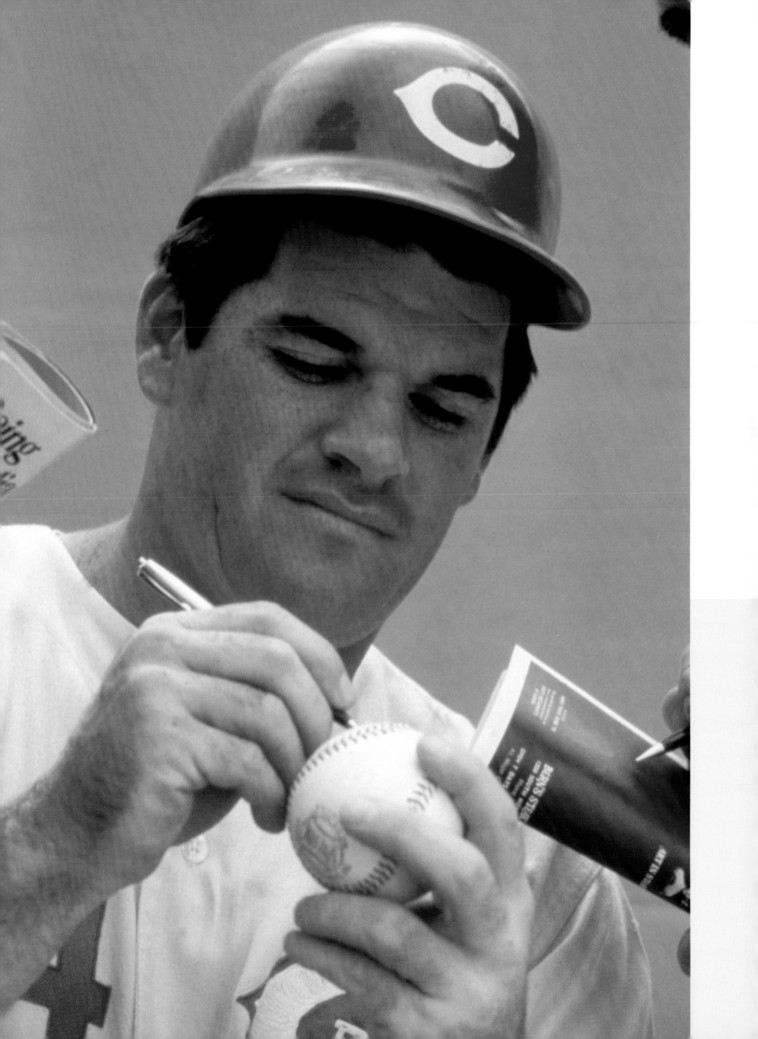

FISHING BUDDIES

Ballplayers traditionally spend around eight weeks at spring training and, naturally, devote most of their time to practice. But hey, there's always a bit of room for "off-campus" fun, as Ozzie discovered. In 1956, just after spring training ended, he instigated his own diversion: He invited four Yankees on a fishing trip. "They didn't rush up north after camp closed," Sweet says. "They had a couple of days off, so I planned some deep-sea fishing." Naturally, he captured the adventure on film. The black-and-white images that resulted are among the most highly regarded in Sweet's catalog. Here's one of the highlights: Mickey Mantle and Billy Martin enjoying a Coke and a smile.

"Billy made the biggest catch, so he did some crowing on board," Ozzie remembers. "There was lot of kidding and needling between the guys, particularly between Billy and Mickey."

THE MANTLES

After retiring during spring training in 1969, Mickey Mantle found time to pose with Mickey Jr. for a photo essay. Among Ozzie's shots: the close-up above, plus a scenic view for *Boys' Life Magazine* of father and son strolling the coastline.

"I remember Mickey and Mickey Jr. as being very close, very natural with each other—and young Mickey for being loaded with freckles," says Ozzie.

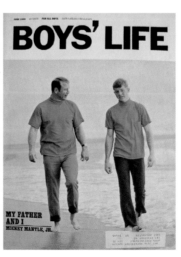

MODEL CITIZENS

In the late 1960s, Sweet had an enticing assignment for All-Star catcher Johnny Bench: pose with a young female model for a clothing advertisement (left). "Johnny did this fashion shoot for me in exchange only for the clothes he was modeling—no fee," says Ozzie. "Can you imagine athletes doing that today?" And in the early 1980s, Sweet got Dave Parker to pose for a magazine spread in his kitchen with his wife.

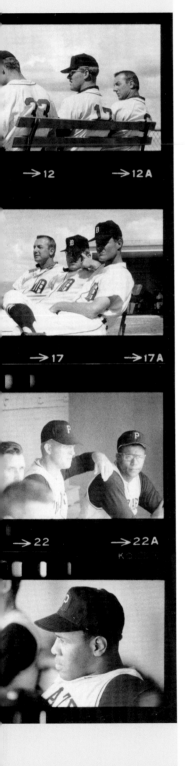

CLASSIC CONTACT

Ozzie's vivid color images of baseball's stars are the ones that catch your eye. But check out this find from Sweet's archives: an unmarked contact sheet from 1968 featuring nearly two dozen black-and-white images of Detroit Tigers and Pittsburgh Pirates players. Although he normally used large-format transparencies at spring training, Sweet occasionally shot black-and-white film. The contact sheet here is packed with spring training atmosphere and noteworthy faces—and even one misfire (Frame 21), which tells us that even the great ones make a mistake now and then.

Taking it from the top (Frame 8), we find the Tigers' Denny McLain resting up before a spring training game. The next image finds McLain watching pre-game warm-ups as the stands start to fill up. In Frame 10, Al Kaline (without hat) gets into the picture with McLain on a bench near the bullpen area. By Frame 11, Kaline has taken a seat, McLain has removed his hat, and Mickey Lolich has popped up in the background. In Frame 12, McLain takes a

seat in between Kaline and, at left, wearing No. 33, rookie Dave Campbell.

In the second row, we get several great looks at Kaline, McLain, and Campbell watching the action, with Lolich loosening his arm in the background. Note the relaxed mood and calm aura these images project, with the shadow of a palm tree (Frames 15 and 16) adding to the effect. The third row finds Sweet still keeping an eye on McLain.

Starting with Frame 22, Sweet has turned his attention to the Pirates. That's Pittsburgh manager Larry Shepard motioning to a player while a bespectacled Bob Veale sits in the background. Frames 23 and 24 feature two more looks at Shepard focusing on the game. And in Frame 25, Sweet captures Roberto Clemente looking as loose as you'll ever see him in a photograph. Frame 26 offers a wonderful profile of the great right fielder, while Frame 27 gives us an equally revealing side view of young Willie Stargell.

In all, this contact sheet serves as a time capsule of sorts—a look inside spring training in an era when players seemed more natural, more human, and more accessible. Yet we also see rare candids of three future Hall of Famers who

boasted otherworldly talents— Kaline (a .297 average with 3,007 hits), Clemente (.317, 3,000 hits), and Stargell (475 HRs and a .282 average). Plus we get a good look at the aces who led Detroit to a World Championship that season. McLain posted a remarkable 31-6 record with a 1.96 ERA and six shutouts in 1968 while Lolich followed a 17-9 regular-season performance with three wins in the World Series. The Pirates' Veale also had an outstanding season: His record in '68 was 13-14, but his ERA was 2.05, third-best in the National League.

We even get a look at a player who would go on to become a respected ESPN announcer and *Baseball Tonight* analyst, Dave Campbell. At the time, "Soup" was a young infielder trying to make the Tigers; he got sent to the minors and then called up late in the season, when he played in nine games and hit his first major league home run.

Here's a view of a throwback ballpark, Bradenton, Fla.'s McKechnie Field, built in 1923 and renovated in the early '90s, as it looks today (left), and as it looked in the mid-1960s (below), when the Kansas City Athletics called it home. The Pirates have trained here since 1969.

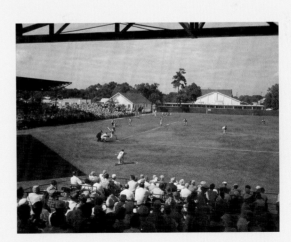

Ozzie used his Florida trips to take all sorts of photographs for calendars. This mid-1960s set-up is one of them.

CHAPTER TWO

PLAY BALL

"*In sports photography, a huge part of your success is luck. The good photographers don't miss when they get lucky. With Ozzie Sweet's work, there was no luck; it was all him. And it was completely wonderful.* "

NEIL LEIFER

PHOTOGRAPHER FOR *SPORTS ILLUSTRATED, TIME, NEWSWEEK, AND LIFE*

Ozzie, the master of the posed-action photograph, got just the right mix of fans (left) for this rah-rah shot from the 1950s.

While he was in the service in the 1940s, Ozzie Sweet developed a photographic style he would put to great use in his future. He called it "simulated action," a technique that allowed him to show the viewer what a war scene might look like.

Sweet's earliest simulated action photographs appeared in *The Range Finder*, the newspaper at Camp Callan near San Diego. In 1941, he sent one of his photographs—a close-up of a soldier in battle, with his teeth clenching a large knife—to *Newsweek*. The editors liked it so much they used it as a cover photo—"my first for a national magazine," Sweet says. "It was early in World War II, and they didn't have battle scenes yet, so I gave them one. I took that image at Camp Callan, using one of my buddies and a huge, shiny blade."

A soldier wouldn't actually have carried a knife with his teeth, Sweet adds with a chuckle. "But I wanted a real daredevil look—like he was out to kill."

When the war ended in 1945, Sweet scored another *Newsweek* cover, this time with a low-angle view of a single Nazi soldier surrendering. Sweet photographed the scene, of course, in America, and he used another friend ("wearing a Nazi uniform we got ahold of") as his subject. When he tripped his camera's shutter, there was absolutely no motion, yet the photograph looked like it was taken on a battlefield in Europe.

When Sweet finished his military duty, *Newsweek* snapped him up as a cover photographer, and in the mid-1940s he produced dozens of eye-catching results. By the time he entered the scene at *SPORT* magazine, he was well practiced. What's more, he had already made two trips to spring training—in 1947 and 1948—for *Newsweek*.

On that first trip to spring training, Sweet surveyed the Cleveland Indians' facility in Tucson and thought, Perfect! With this landscape, he could use the same principles in baseball that he employed with his wartime photographs: a creative concept, a controlled setting, and a perfectly still subject "in action."

"In sports photography, a huge part of your success is luck," says Neil Leifer, himself a top name in the field, with decades worth of cover and interior credits in *Sports Illustrated*, *Time*, *Newsweek*, and *Life*, among many others. "The good photographers don't miss when they get lucky. With Ozzie Sweet's work, there was no luck; it was all him. And it was completely wonderful.

"I like taking pictures that I can control; all photographers do," Leifer adds. "Ozzie had total control."

The big question with Sweet's simulated action technique was: Could he get the day's biggest sports stars to "act"? In other words, he knew he could control everything except the subject's actions (okay, and the weather, too—but the odds in Florida and Arizona were always in his favor). But if he could also reduce the "margin for error," so to speak, by somehow getting reasonable cooperation from his subjects, he'd be golden.

So he developed a process and put it to the test. First, he strived to take no more than 20 minutes of a player's time, if he could help it. His camera, lights, and backdrops were set up and ready so that when the subject arrived, he'd enjoy an in-and-out experience.

Second, Sweet used his abilities as a director to guide his subject. Telling a player to "swing the bat" wasn't enough; in his classic simulated action photographs, Sweet would show the player what he wanted, coax him into particular stopped-action poses, and encourage him to try for the right expression.

Third, Sweet would rely on his own natural gift for reading human nature—the personalities, moods, and idiosyncrasies of those he photographed. The key: building relationships. Over the course of a few years, players began to recognize Sweet, and he developed a rapport with them. He knew how "painless" a session would have to be or, conversely, how far he could push a player (and how far he could push the envelope, too, in terms of concept). He knew a Luis Aparicio would "perform"—and enjoy it—whereas a Joe DiMaggio might be less tolerant.

Even with all of those factors in place, Sweet still had to execute. And that's where his preparation, concepts, and ability to visualize came into play. He'd plan out in his mind the types of plays—big swings, windups, pivots—you'd see in baseball.

"He clearly understands the game," Leifer says. "So if it was Mickey Mantle swinging, it looked real—even though you knew the camera can't be on the ground, with that blue sky behind Mickey. Ozzie always had the angle right. If it was Warren Spahn's leg kick, you knew it wasn't real action, but Ozzie had Spahn's motion just right."

Adds Richard Johnson, curator of the New England Sport Museum, "Ozzie made those simulated action images work. Sometimes other photographers would do those types of images, but they'd come off as serious. Ozzie's often had a tongue-in-cheek quality, and therefore a charm that others lack. His subjects always seemed to have fun with what they did, and Ozzie captured that."

Certain players cooperated more readily than others, and when you study Sweet's archives, the "stars" stand out. We've compiled the cream of the crop in this chapter. Just call 'em "Ozzie's All-Stars"—the players who worked hardest to help him create photographs that "sold" the action.

LOU BROCK, LF

Leading off is the man who made the St. Louis Cardinals' offense tick in the 1960s and '70s. Sweet captured Brock in poses that reflected his specialty: stealing bases. He had 938 of them, a mark he held until Rickey Henderson broke it in 1991. Brock was no slouch with the bat, either: He had 3,023 hits and a .293 career average.

In this startlingly clear photograph Sweet shows Brock leading off first base, his eyes trained on the pitcher's every move. The image dates to spring 1968.

"What a wonderfully cooperative guy—it seemed like Lou enjoyed working with me and the camera as much as he enjoyed playing ball," says Ozzie.

"His subjects always seemed to have fun with what they did, and Ozzie captured that."

JACKIE ROBINSON, 2B

Behind Brock we have Jackie Robinson of the Dodgers. Ozzie made him look almost majestic in a classic 1949 hitting pose (right). For the vintage image below, Sweet got Robinson to "slide" into home, arms up, a look of strain on this face. In reality, of course, he's not moving at all. An alternate angle appeared on the cover of *SPORT's* October 1951 issue. Sweet, in his 1958 book *My Camera Pays Off,* wrote of the session: "I shot Jackie Robinson in one of his fabulous slides by building a one-legged stool to prop him in a flying position, using wood ashes instead of dust so that a healthy kick raised a realistic cloud. When we had finished working in our private dust bowl, a deep layer of ashes had settled on all of us, but it was worth the discomfort and hours we spent cleaning every inch of equipment, because the results appeared as truly believable action."

At the time, Robinson was in the midst of his Hall of Fame career. He was coming off seasons in which he hit .342 and .328; in 1951, he'd go on to hit .338 with 19 HRs, 25 steals, and 106 runs. He played for five more seasons after that, retiring at age 37 with a career average of .311.

MICKEY MANTLE, CF
Sweet was already shooting
SPORT covers when Mantle
began his rookie season with
the Yankees in 1951. He would
become a regular in front of
Sweet's camera for years to
come, so the two developed a
real camaraderie. "Every year,"
Sweet recalls, "he'd see me
show up at spring training and
he'd yell out, 'Hey Ozz, what
kind of crazy thing are we
gonna do this year?'" Mantle
was especially effective as a
subject, Sweet says, because
he took it seriously. One of
Ozzie's favorites is pictured
here, a photograph that dates
to spring 1960. Instead of
creating a standard batting
pose, Sweet added a catcher
and umpire to complement
Mantle, who stood as if he were
awaiting a pitch.

Pulling it all together took
hours of planning, "but the
actual photography took
20 minutes," Sweet says.
"And the whole session
wouldn't have been worth a
damn without Mickey's
expression."

"Hey Ozz, what kind of crazy thing are we gonna do this year?"

DUKE SNIDER, LF

Batting cleanup is The Duke, another frequent Sweet subject. Snider posed in a variety of simulated action photographs over the years, including the batting stance below that dates to the early 1950s, when Snider was hitting his prime. At left, Ozzie got the All-Star center fielder to demonstrate his defensive prowess, simulating a leaping catch at the wall for a photograph that appeared on the September, 1955 cover of *SPORT*.

"I remember driving to photograph Duke Snider at Vero Beach for a cover," says Ozzie. "I passed by all kinds of citrus groves, and I was allergic to something in the air. By the time I arrived to take his picture, I was weeping, my eyes were all red, and I was a mess—I looked really sick. And Duke said, 'You must have had a wild party last night!'"

"I was weeping, my eyes were all red, and I was a mess—I looked really sick. And Duke said, 'You must have had a wild party last night!'"

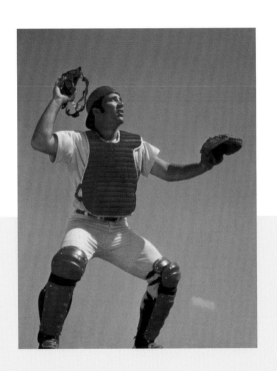

JOHNNY BENCH, C

Hitting fifth is the Reds'
cannon-armed catcher, shown
in full gear in a pair of images
dating to the early 1970s. By
dangling a ball on a string and
tapping it to create movement
(above), Ozzie created a
pitcher's view of Bench. At the
time, Bench was emerging as
baseball's top-hitting catcher;
his 1970 season is one of the
best ever by a backstop: 45
home runs, 148 RBI, and a
.293 average. He played 17
seasons, all with the Reds, and
had 389 home runs, 2,048
hits, and a .267 average.

WILLIE STARGELL, 1B

Batting behind Bench is our first baseman, Willie Stargell. This gentle giant was patient and cooperative with Sweet for a number of poses, one of which is presented here: Stargell fielding his position with one of those classic three-fingered first-baseman's mitts. Sweet took this photograph from below, with Stargell standing atop sand he had piled on a board that was propped up by two sawhorses. The image dates to spring 1968, when Stargell, at 28, was just entering his prime. His best season would come in 1971, when he helped Pittsburgh to a World Series title by hitting .295 with 48 homers and 125 RBI. Eight years later, at age 39, he was voted co-MVP of the NL (with Keith Hernandez) after hitting 32 homers to lead Pittsburgh to another World Series win. Stargell would play for 21 seasons, all with Pittsburgh, and hit 475 home runs, tying him with Stan Musial.

BROOKS ROBINSON, 3B

Batting seventh in our lineup is arguably the best-fielding third baseman ever. This photograph of Robinson is a perfect example of how Sweet's controlled set-ups allowed him to accomplish the highest-quality photographs. Look at the tack-sharp detail in Brooks' hat and uniform. Sweet took the image in spring 1967; a few months earlier, Robinson had helped lead the Orioles to a sweep over the Dodgers in the 1966 World Series.

"Brooks was friendly and talkative and made you feel comfortable—none of that 'gotta-get-this-done' nervous tension," says Ozzie.

Robinson's career would span 23 seasons and he'd bat .267 with 268 home runs, winning an AL Most Valuable Player award along the way (1964) plus a World Series MVP award (1970). But it was his meticulous fielding that made him special: He won 16 Gold Gloves.

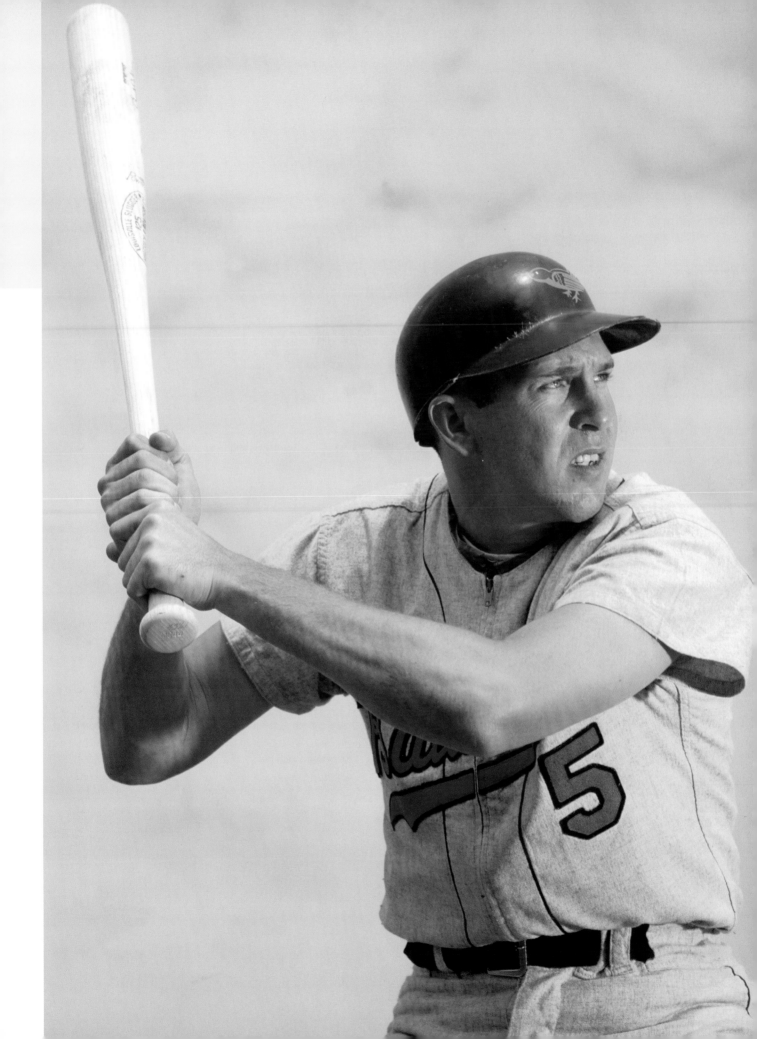

LUIS APARICIO, SS

Our eighth hitter, Aparicio, was one of Sweet's favorite subjects. "He loved doing those sessions" Ozzie says. "He was enthusiastic and upbeat, always willing to perform in front of the camera." As a player, Aparicio was equally effective—a steady slap hitter who could create havoc on the base paths (506 steals) and win games with his glove. In 1960, Sweet had Aparicio pose in a variety of photographs that look like honest action; the best of a stunning lot is the classic photo (top, left), where Aparicio seems to be suspended in air. In fact, he was standing "dead still," says Ozzie.

"Not only was Luis one of my favorite subjects, but he also was the most dramatic," says Ozzie. "No matter what I'd ask him to do, he'd do it—and do it so well that it would look absolutely honest."

SANDY KOUFAX, P

He was not only the best pitcher in the game during his playing days, but Koufax was a Sweet favorite and a regular subject. "Sandy was a little bit moody, but that doesn't mean he wasn't cooperative," Ozzie remembers. "He'd listen and give you what you wanted—he was never a problem."

The image at left—Koufax looking toward his catcher for the sign—dates to spring 1965. At the time, he was in the midst of a stretch during which he was downright nasty on the mound; his ERAs from 1963 through 1966 were 1.88, 1.74, 2.04, and 1.73. He was anything but nasty in front of Sweet's camera, however. With Koufax, Ozzie always knew what he'd get: a cooperative spirit and honest effort.

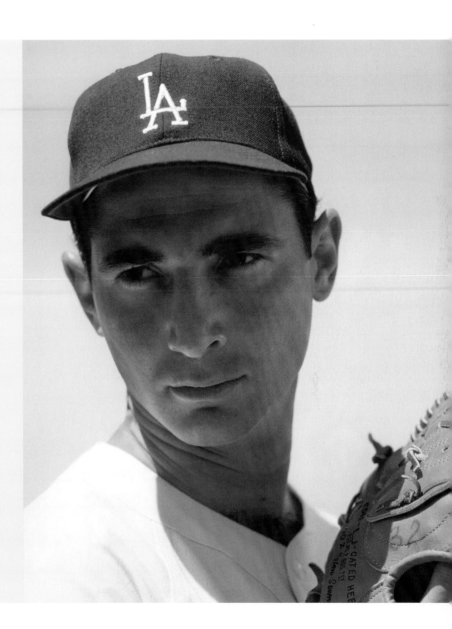

"Sandy was a little bit moody, but that doesn't mean he wasn't cooperative."

WHITEY FORD, P

The Yankees' frequent appearances in the World Series in the 1950s kept Sweet coming back to the team's training camp. There, he often focused on Ford, pictured at right conferring with a catcher and, left, simulating a pitch. Ford's winning percentage over his 16-year career was .690—not surprising when you consider that his lifetime ERA was 2.75. In postseason play, he was just as consistent: a 2.71 ERA in 22 starts.

"I remember shooting Whitey pretty often as a player," says Ozzie. "But one of the sessions I remember most was at the beach, where I photographed him playing in the sand with his wife and small children."

WARREN SPAHN, P

Sweet's close-up of Spahn is a lesson in how to look a runner back to a base. The cold, hard stare that Spahn is giving to an imaginary runner on second is also a testament to Sweet's knack for eliciting convincing expressions. "Warren looks very serious here, but this is just real fine acting," says Ozzie. "That's just a camera out there that he's looking at—not a base-runner!"

The photo dates to 1952, the year before the Boston Braves moved to Milwaukee. Spahn was coming off a 22-win season, one of 13 times he'd win 20 games.

ROBIN ROBERTS, P

Sweet photographed Roberts frequently in the 1950s, and with good reason. The hard-throwing right-hander had six straight 20-win seasons from 1950 through 1955. Here we see Roberts looking serious and competitive as Sweet, shooting from an extreme low angle, emphasizes his big windup.

EWELL BLACKWELL, P

At times, Sweet would hang a ball on a string and nudge it to give it movement, and then he'd position a pitcher behind it, arm extended. You saw it earlier with Whitey Ford; here it is again with the lanky Blackwell, a 22-game winner for the Reds in 1947. This photograph dates to the early 1950s, when he had 17- and 16-win seasons. Injuries, however, curtailed his career; he retired in 1955 after winning 82 games in his 10 years.

RALPH TERRY, P

The hero of the 1962 World Series, Terry won Games 5 and 7 (the latter a four-hit shutout) as the Yankees edged the Giants. Ozzie was still in a mood to celebrate when camp opened in 1963, so he enlisted three young pitchers—from left, Roland Sheldon, Hal Stowe, and Jim Bronstad—to hoist Terry onto their shoulders to reenact the Game 7 celebration (right). "None of these guys are actors, but they put on a convincing performance," says Ozzie.

Terry was noted for a high leg kick that was a distraction to batters, so Sweet emphasized it in the simulated delivery photographs on this page.

LOU BOUDREAU, PLAYER-MANAGER

A sure-handed shortstop and tremendous hitter, Boudreau was the Indians player-manager for nine seasons. Ozzie got Boudreau to strike this thinking-man's pose during spring training in 1948. Little did either man know that Boudreau was on the verge of a season for the ages. The manager batted .355, with 18 homers and 106 RBIs, while leading the AL in fielding average. In a one-game playoff against the Red Sox, Boudreau had four hits, including two homers, in an 8-3 win that sent the Indians into the World Series, where they defeated the Boston Braves.

PAUL RICHARDS, MANAGER

So he never won a championship as manager of the White Sox (1951 through '54, plus a lone "comeback" season in 1976) or the Orioles (1955 through '61). Even so, Richards (below) makes our team for his wild-eyed performance. During the session, done at spring training in 1961, Sweet asked Richards to "go at it" with an umpire and Richards complied, looking irate and a little on edge—and also a bit like he might smile.

FRANKIE FRISCH, COACH

This Hall of Fame second baseman (right) had an outstanding career beginning in 1919 for the New York Giants and ending in 1937 for the Cardinals. As player/manager, he led the "Gas House Gang" Cardinals to a World Series title in 1934 and to second-place finishes in 1935 and '36. He also managed Pittsburgh (from 1940 through 1946) and the Cubs (1949 through 1951), as well as spending one year as a coach with the Giants. It was during 1948 spring training that Sweet took this memorable photograph of the still-competitive Frisch barking instructions.

THE BENCH

Sweet's simulated action archives are deep enough that we're able to complement our starting team with a talented bench, as evidenced on the following pages.

First up, Ozzie gets second baseman Charlie Neal (right) to hang tough in the face of a sliding runner. Neal was an All-Star for the Dodgers in 1959 and '60.

Joe Pepitone (below), noted for a powerful swing that brought him 28 home runs and 100 RBIs in 1964, was happy to demonstrate his follow-through for Ozzie.

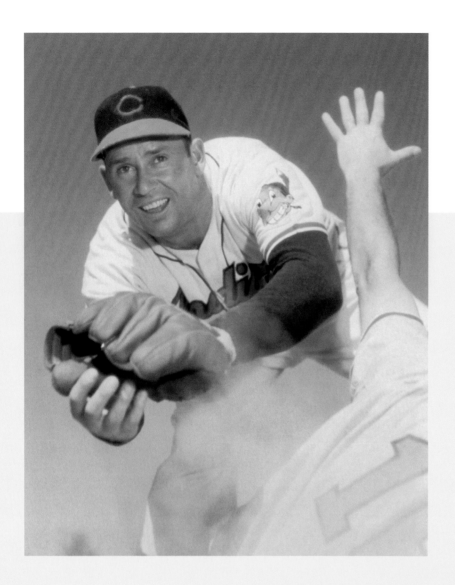

TWO HANDERS

In one of Sweet's first simulated action images involving a baseball player (it dates to 1949), the Indians' Joe Gordon (left) shows his two-handed technique at second base. Below, we get a look at Pee Wee Reese locking in on a pop fly. (Listen hard enough and you can still hear dads telling their kids: "See—use two hands when you catch those fly balls, just like Pee Wee does.") Minnie Minoso (opposite page) was more noted for his bat, so Ozzie got him to pose at the finale of a mighty swing in 1954.

TRESH TALK

After hitting 25 home runs in 1963, Yankee outfielder Tom Tresh was on Ozzie's radar the following spring. The slugger settled into his stance (right) and, with Ozzie shooting from a low angle, became larger than life. Tresh also gave Ozzie a look at his follow through (above).

TWIN KILLER

In 1965, Tony Oliva hit .321 to win his second consecutive AL batting crown while helping the Twins win the World Series. The next spring, he struck the confident pose of a slugger for Ozzie's camera. Ozzie also created a low-angle photograph (above) that shows how Oliva might have appeared to a catcher looking up the first-base line.

REAL SWINGERS

Ozzie was always on the lookout
for talent. He found it in the
person of Tommy Davis (right),
who had won two consecutive
NL batting crowns when Ozzie
caught up with him in 1964.
Frank Howard (below) twice led
the NL in home runs, and
caught Ozzie's eye by hitting 23
in his first full season, 1960.

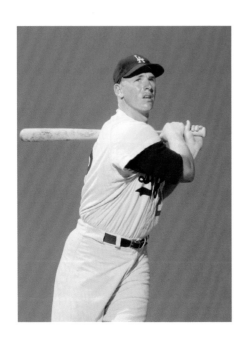

BIG BOPPERS

We fill out "Ozzie's All-Stars" with two Red Sox outfielders, Fred Lynn (bottom) and Tony Conigliaro (left). They're shown here in fielding poses but they were known first for their sticks. Lynn, in his 17-year career with Boston, California, Baltimore, Detroit, and San Diego, hit 306 homers and batted .283. "Tony C" burst onto the scene with 24 home runs in 1964, followed by seasons of 32, 28, and 20 before fate stepped in. On Aug. 18, 1967, he got hit in his left eye with a Jack Hamilton fastball. He missed all of 1968 but put on an inspiring comeback in 1969, hitting 20 home runs. He followed that season with a career-best 36 in 1970. Traded to California in 1971, Conigliaro's career fizzled and he retired at age 26. A 1975 comeback attempt with Boston lasted only until June.

CHAPTER THREE

THE SPLENDID MANAGER

"In 1969 the players were thrilled and probably somewhat intimidated by Williams. He brought double or triple the media coverage they'd ever experienced in spring training."

PHIL WOOD

JOURNALIST AND RADIO ANNOUNCER

Ozzie delighted in using his semi-submersible camera to take humorous photos, such as this one showing a fish eluding the net of an anonymous fisherman.

Major League Baseball made headlines late in the 2004 season by announcing —after months of speculation—that it was returning to Washington, D.C. by uprooting the Montreal Expos and moving the franchise nearly 500 miles south. The story inspired a nostalgia blitz as fans and media alike revisited the history of baseball in our nation's capital.

The last time we saw big-league baseball in Washington, of course, was 1971 and the Senators' manager was Ted Williams. "The Splendid Splinter" had taken over the job in 1969, nine years after he played his final season. In signing with the Senators, he walked into a challenging (to say the least) situation, inheriting a team with a history of losing.

The original Senators played in Washington from 1901 through 1960; in those six decades, the franchise posted a record above .500 only 16 times. In 1961, the team moved to Minnesota and became the Twins. The same season, D.C. won a replacement franchise: the expansion Washington Senators. The new team got off to a horrendous start, losing at least 100 games per season from 1961 through 1964. They were only slightly better the next three seasons (70-92, 71-88, and 76-85) but regressed in 1968 (65-96).

Then along came Ted Williams. In his first season, he made an immediate impact, leading the 1969 Senators to an 86-76 record—21 wins more than the previous season. "In 1969 the players were thrilled and probably somewhat intimidated by Williams," recalls Phil Wood, a longtime journalist and radio announcer in the Baltimore/Washington area. "He brought

double or triple the media coverage they'd ever experienced in spring training."

Understandably, spirits were high going into the 1970 season. Unfortunately, the Senators had a relapse, drooping to 70-92. Things got worse in 1971: The Senators posted a 63-96 record in front of smaller and smaller crowds at Robert F. Kennedy Stadium. With the franchise losing money as quickly as it lost games, owner Bob Short moved the team in 1972 to Texas, where the Senators became the Rangers. The move didn't help. Texas stumbled through a 54-100 campaign in '72, Williams' final year as manager.

"Ted was quite dramatic as a manager," Ozzie recalls. "When he got his players together, he'd hold their attention using his hands and loud voice. He wanted input, too, so he'd ask his players if they had anything to add, or if they had any questions. He wanted more of a conversation than a lecture."

But let's not dwell on the negative. Let's return to spring training 1969, when optimism filled the hearts of Washington fans. No, it wouldn't be easy for Ted Williams—or anyone—to turn this team around. The Senators of '68 suffered from generous pitching and a porous defense, and they were particularly pathetic at the plate, batting .224 as a team. The only real threat was huge Frank Howard, the 6-foot-7, 255-pound outfielder/first baseman who blasted 44 home runs in '68. The Senators' faithful, however, had high hopes, buoyed by the arrival of the last man to hit .400 in a season.

Williams got things rolling in Pompano Beach, Fla., where the Senators trained.

TWO STARS

Ozzie was among the press members on hand at the Senators' camp in 1969. He had photographed Williams often in the past, dating to the early 1950s, and had earned his respect. Their first meeting was at spring training in 1951; Sweet, shooting for *SPORT*, arranged a portrait session with the Red Sox star at the team's Sarasota, Fla., facility. On the day of the shoot, Sweet arrived early, as always, and set up his view camera, equipment, and backdrops. Ted, however, never showed up at the portable studio. Sweet returned the next day, hoping Ted would squeeze in a few minutes. No luck. Finally, on the third day, Sweet recalls, "Ted must have noticed me, and how I kept coming back." Williams approached Sweet and sat for a series of photographs that produced perhaps the best Williams portrait ever taken (see page 139).

Because of their history, Williams gave Sweet ample time in 1969 for a series of portraits (right) that still stand as remarkable records of Ted's first days as a manager. The large photo here appeared on the June 1969 cover of *SPORT*. It's a study in intensity, with Williams looking all business on the dugout steps.

"Ted was quite dramatic as a manager."

*"Ted must have noticed me, and
how I kept coming back."*

TED AT WORK

Just as interesting as Sweet's portraits of Williams is a wonderful series of Sweet candids showing Ted at work—photographs that illustrate how expressive he was. The best examples are presented here; most have never been published. In taking these images, Sweet explains, "I didn't interfere at all... There was no simulated action here, no directing—I was just shooting as it happened."

The series includes a photograph of a smiling

"He had this booming voice...Everyone around him could hear what he was saying."

Williams leaning against a batting cage, focusing on his hitters' swings, and another where he's barking instructions. In the third photo (opposite page, top), we see Ted having a heart-to-heart with Brant Alyea, an outfielder who would increase his home run total from 6 in 1968 to 11 under Williams. Alyea was shipped to Minnesota for the 1970 season, where his time with Williams paid more dividends: He had his best season, batting .291 with 16 home runs.

Above, Williams is evaluating Del Unser, a young outfielder. Put yourself in Unser's shoes: You're a 24-year-old, second-year player who had plenty of playing time in your rookie season (156 games), yet you batted only .230 with a meager .282 on-base percentage. In 635 at-bats, you hit just one home run, and your slugging percentage was just .277. Now here you are showing your swing to Ted Williams, who used to pile up more extra-base hits in a month than you had in your entire first season. That's pressure! And judging from

Unser's face in the next photograph in the series (below), he felt the pressure. Unser's expression can only be interpreted as, "Whew!"as Williams turns his attention to No. 54, Tom Grieve, the Senators' No. 1 pick in the 1966 draft who failed to make the team as a 20-year-old under Williams, but went on to a 10-year big-league career and later became the Rangers' GM. For Unser, the attention from Williams paid off. He increased his average in 1969 by 56 points to .286.

THE TEACHER

One of Ted Williams' main projects in 1969 was Mike Epstein, the 6-foot-3, 230 pound first baseman with a big swing and big strikeout total. He was acquired from the Orioles early in the 1967 season but hit only .226 with 9 homers—and 79 strikeouts. He improved marginally in 1968 to .234, 13 HRs, and 91 whiffs.

Sweet captured a series of photographs of the two at work and it speaks volumes about Williams' intensity. In the first image note that Williams is wearing sunglasses as he instructs Epstein, who's wearing No. 12 (he switched to No. 6 during the regular season). In the second image, Williams has removed his sunglasses for better eye-to-eye contact and appears to be exploring a flaw in Epstein's swing. In the third photograph, Williams is showing a bat to Epstein as if to say, "This is a bat. And this is the end that you hold." In the fourth image, Ted shows how, demonstrating his swing.

The personal attention paid off: Epstein hit .278 with 30 homers in 1969. He wasn't the only one to benefit. Frank Howard went from 141 strikeouts to 96 while adding 20-plus points to his batting average. Ed Brinkman, who'd batted below .200 in the previous two years, hit .266 and .262 under Williams, while Williams helped outfielder Hank Allen improve his average from .219 to .277.

"There was no simulated action here, no directing—I was just shooting as it happened."

THE GENERAL

Behind Williams, the Senators finished five games over .500 in 1969, but reverted to their losing ways in 1970—finishing 11 games under .500. As spring training '71 opened, Sweet headed back to Pompano Beach to photograph Williams and his revamped team. Among the new images he captured is a striking ground-level view of Ted, with his booming voice, addressing his players at practice.

NEW FACES

After their disappointing 1970 season, the Senators made a number of moves, including trades that brought Denny McLain and Curt Flood to Washington for the 1971 season. Sweet grabbed photographs of Williams during private time with both McLain (left) and Flood (opposite page). The '71 Sweet sessions also included a formal portrait of Williams, McLain, and Flood (below) for *SPORT*'s May 1971 cover.

Despite their off-season additions, the Senators finished 15 games under .500. Indeed, McLain was a major bust in D.C., posting a 10-22 record. He played one more season, bouncing from Oakland to Atlanta, and then got released by the Braves, just before his 29th birthday, near the end of spring training 1973. Flood played in only 13 games in 1971 due to injuries, retiring after the season at age 33. But his place in baseball was secure due to his challenge of baseball's old reserve clause rule, which bound a player to one team indefinitely. Flood's resolve led to the end of the reserve clause—and to the birth of free agency.

It was unfortunate for Williams' managerial career that McLain and Flood fizzled. But, despite several poor trades by the Senators' front office, Williams remained stoic in a tough situation, as the candid studies below illustrate.

FAN FAVORITE

In the Senators' last hurrah in Washington, on Sept. 30, 1971 at RFK Stadium, the team suffered a forfeit loss to the Yankees. It was prompted by swarms of fans—angry over owner Bob Short's decision to move their team to Texas— storming the field in the ninth inning with the Senators leading by two runs. Immediately following the game, Williams told reporters he'd go to Texas when the franchise moved in 1972, and he did, but he stayed for only a year.

Sweet prefers to remember the positive, however. And his photographs do just that: They remind us of Williams' successes—especially with regard to his influence on his hitters—rather than the losses. Without a doubt, Williams was a convincing batting coach, Sweet says. "He got his point across," he recalls. "He had that loud, booming voice, so everyone within earshot could hear what he was saying."

Perhaps none of Sweet's images from Pompano Beach are as arresting as those of Williams signing autographs for young fans in 1971. Who could have been more hopeful than these young believers?

In the early 1980s, around a dozen years after Williams' managerial experience with the Senators and Rangers ended, Sweet's camera caught up with Ted as a Red Sox hitting instructor (opposite page).

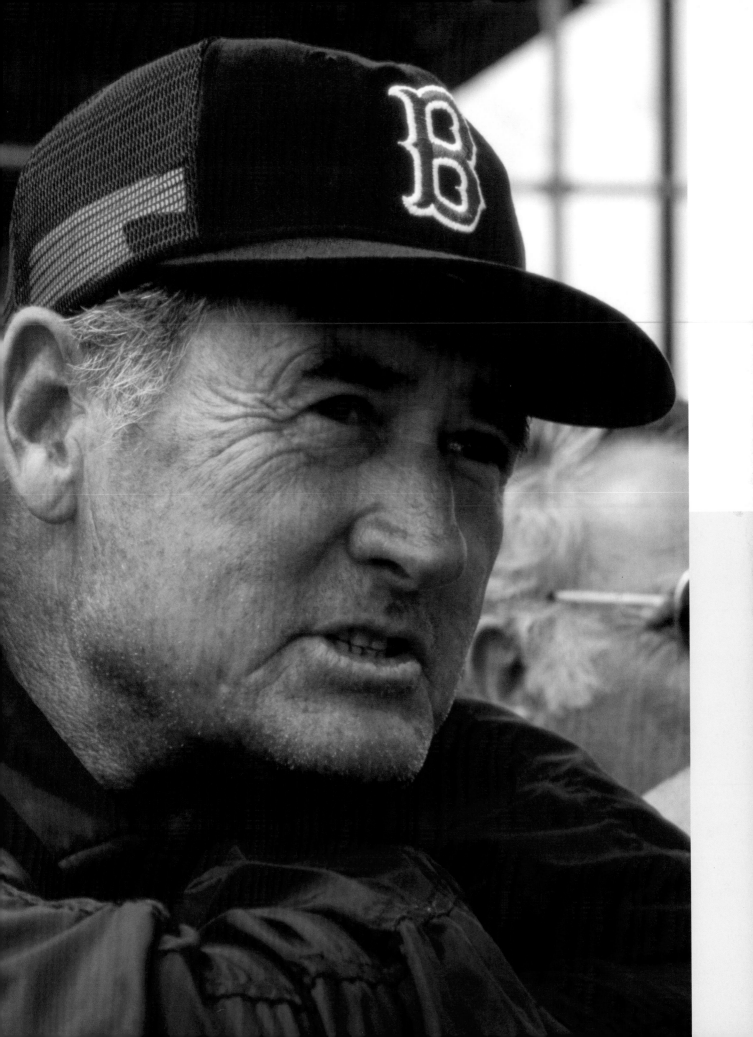

CHAPTER FOUR

THEY SMILED FOR MY CAMERA

"If you want a cocky, semi-sardonic look on a champ's face, tell him a corny gag."

OZZIE

Ozzie used a self-built contraption he called "the semi-sub" to take this late 1960s photograph. Inside the semi-sub, his camera remained dry while Ozzie photographed his subject.

113

"I always had a list of one-liners—and
they had to be one-liners because you
didn't have time to tell long jokes."

"Masters of portraiture are those who have a sincere interest in people, who understand human nature and bring out the inner personality of the subject."

If ever a photographer has lived by those words, it's Ozzie Sweet—which is appropriate, because he wrote them in his 1958 book *My Camera Pays Off*. He also explained that for most people, "a portrait sitting is painful." And he hears, over and over, the phrase "Be careful; my face will break your camera...."

In dealing with self-conscious subjects, Sweet's strategy in his early years was (as it is now) to "make them momentarily forget themselves, the camera, the lights, and the photographer." In other words, distract the subject—whether it's a man, woman, or child. Or a baseball star. Most athletes, after all, are no different than anyone else when it comes to sitting in front of a camera. They rank it up there with a visit to the dentist.

How does Sweet distract the self-conscious? He engages. He asks questions. He works in bits of small talk—and works out his running inventory of jokes. During his heyday of the late 1940s through the 1960s, he says, "I always had a list of one-liners—and they had to be one-liners because you didn't have time to tell long jokes." (Did you hear about the fly that landed on the toilet seat—and got pissed off?)

Sweet's sense of humor has allowed him to connect with all types of players—the impatient, the apprehensive, the surly, the shy. It also allowed him to prompt natural smiles out of just about everyone he photographed. And make no mistake: It isn't easy to get smiles out of ballplayers. Here's another passage from Sweet's *My Camera Pays Off*: "Unfreezing stiff faces is a problem most often met in working with the sports celebs.... If you want a cocky, semi-sardonic look on a champ's face, tell him a corny gag. I once loosened up Ted Williams with this cornball:

'What is green all over and has wheels?' Answer: 'Grass—I was lying about the wheels.' I'll never forget the look Ted was giving me as I tripped the shutter."

Richard Johnson, curator of the New England Museum of Sports, didn't have the pleasure of watching Sweet's old photo sessions take place, but in studying the images, he envisions what went on. "I'm sure he made people laugh," Johnson says. "He was probably clowning around; he probably had 10 jokes that he'd keep and throw out at just the right time. Athletes are used to the banter of the locker room; the impression of Ozzie I get is, he's a charmer but he's also a man's man. He wouldn't have any trouble talking about hunting, fishing, drinking, carousing, card-playing. He'd put people at ease.

"The whole thing with Ozzie's work is, everybody's happy," Johnson adds. "I've never seen a portrait of his where someone has a game face on; they have their 'post-game' face."

Sweet had other secrets, too. "I never ask a subject to look at the camera and I never say 'Hold it,'" he wrote in *My Camera Pays Off*. "I never ask for a smile because I know it would be forced."

Look through the gallery of portraits in this chapter and you'll find few hints of "forced." Consider Ozzie's classic 1956 portrait of the Boys of Summer (opposite page): five Brooklyn Dodgers, having finally beaten the Yankees in the World Series, smiling in sync. (From left, that's Carl Erskine, Gil Hodges, Pee Wee Reese, Jackie Robinson, and Duke Snider.)

"When photographing a group, someone always seems to close his eyes, or he can't seem to time his smile with the others," Ozzie says. "I was lucky with 'Boys of Summer.' All the smiles are great. And it took only five exposures."

The four-dozen smiles on these pages are natural and timeless, and Sweet himself is still drawn to them, even after all these years. If there's one chapter between the two covers of this book that most attracts Ozzie (and most reflects him), it's this one: all smiles.

SMILING EYES

We've arranged the faces in this chapter alphabetically, which works perfectly because it puts Luis Aparicio first among individual players. And if Sweet had to select just one smiling face for this chapter, it would have been Aparicio. With a glove, he had few peers. Smooth as silk, wide-ranging, quick release, strong arm—he had it all, which is why Casey Stengel once said of him, "If that kid gets any better, you might as well call in the second baseman and third baseman because he gobbles up everything within a mile of him." Aparicio won nine Gold Glove awards, including five in a row from 1958 through 1962, and was a 10-time All-Star. He was no liability on offense, either. In 18 seasons he amassed 2,677 hits, struck out only 742 times in 10,230 at-bats, stole 506 bases, and scored 1,335 runs.

The upbeat, energetic Aparicio also turned in stellar work for Sweet, as evident on these two pages. In particular, Ozzie has a real fondness for the 1962 portrait on the opposite page. "This is the greatest of all smiles," Sweet says. "It's kind of a scallywag smile—nice and natural and genuine. If you study the picture, even his eyes seem to smile and sparkle. It's one of my favorites."

"It's kind of a scallywag smile— nice and natural and genuine."

AW SHUCKS

Sweet showed an ability to capture a subject's personality well before—and well after—the Aparicio session. He drew an appropriately "shy" smile out of Ewell Blackwell (left) in 1951, while his Lou Brock (below), from 1968, is a mix of self-conscious and affable.

QUIET CONFIDENCE

In photographing the Phillies' Johnny Callison in 1965, Sweet achieved a relaxed but serious look. The confident expression is befitting of the steady outfielder, who quietly hit 226 homers in a 16-year career.

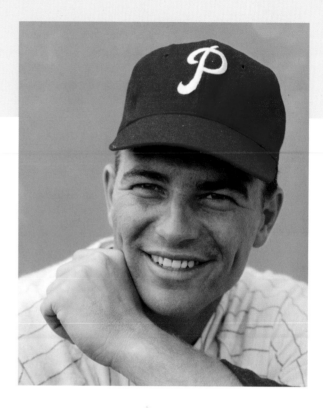

ALL SMILES

Tommy Davis (left) had plenty to grin about in 1963. His smile here, in a simulated action photograph with Ron Fairly and Willie Davis, may have had something to do with his phenomenal 1962 season, when he hit .346 with 230 hits, 27 home runs, and 153 RBI.

When Sweet photographed Leo Durocher (bottom) in 1950, he got a "nice guy" smile out of the scrappy New York Giants manager. Durocher, a 1994 Hall of Fame inductee, was a light-hitting shortstop from 1925 through 1945 (.247 with 24 home runs). He became better known as a manager, serving as skipper of the Dodgers, Giants, Cubs, and Astros between 1939 and 1973. His nickname sums up his feisty persona: "Leo the Lip."

Nelson "Nellie" Fox (below)—cap tilted and cheek full of chaw—gave Sweet a disarming smile in this 1957 portrait. The White Sox second baseman was at the top of his game in the late 1950s, hitting over .300 three consecutive years (1957 through 1959) and winning the AL MVP award in '59.

Whitey Ford (right) is shown in a bright 1963 photograph that featured "honest sweat," as Sweet calls it. Ford had one of his finest seasons in 1963, posting a 24-7 record and a 2.74 ERA.

STEADY AS SHE GOES

Detroit pitcher Ned Garver and Baltimore first baseman Jim Gentile weren't the biggest stars Sweet ever photographed, but both were steady big-leaguers who produced some memorable seasons. Garver (bottom) looks loose and carefree in a 1955 portrait. The Gentile portrait (below) appeared in the August 1963 issue of *SPORT*, which tapped "Diamond Jim" as a top AL star, per a "secret poll" of managers.

If Sweet captured a warm smile from Gentile, he got a sparkling one from Mudcat

Grant (left) in spring 1966. The previous season, everything went right for Grant—a 21-7 record, 3.30 ERA, six shutouts, and two World Series wins (although his Twins lost the Fall Classic to the Dodgers).

Tommy Henrich's hat-tipping smile (below) dates to spring 1949, when the Yankee outfielder/first baseman was about to embark on his last productive season (24 home runs and 85 RBI). The following February, *SPORT* used the image on its cover, but the season that followed, 1950, turned out to be Henrich's last.

Ozzie Sweet loved to work young fans into his photographs. Here, we see a contented-looking Harmon Killebrew surrounded by four excited boys. Sweet took this portrait in 1960 at spring training following Killebrew's first full season in the majors. In 1959, he hit 42 home runs to launch a Hall of Fame career that included 573 home runs. Despite his nickname "Killer," Killebrew was a gentle personality, as this portrait reflects.

In another image that combines slugger with young admirer, Ralph Kiner (left) looks as happy as his awe-struck batboy. No wonder: Kiner hit 54 home runs with 127 RBI the season before, 1949, and would hit 47 more in 1950. He played for only 10 seasons but finished with 369 home runs and a spot in the Hall of Fame.

A CUT ABOVE

Ted Kluszewski was known almost as much for his cut-off sleeves as for his impressive home runs. He once told a writer, "We had those flannel uniforms, and every time I'd swing the bat, my arms would get hung up on the sleeves. I complained about it, but they [the Reds' management] hemmed and hawed and finally I took a pair of scissors and cut them off ... it was either that or change my swing, and I wasn't going to change my swing."

Kluszewski was an Ozzie favorite. "There are guys who would cut loose and laugh easily," Ozzie remembers, "and Klu was one of them. He had a nice smile and eyes that laughed as well."

"There are guys who would cut loose and laugh easily, and Klu was one of them."

"I've shot Mickey in many situations, including on a fishing boat that almost turned over."

MICK-HAPPY TIMES

The best smile this side of Luis Aparicio, in Ozzie Sweet's eye, was Mickey Mantle's. On these pages, we get a look at the evolution of The Mick's smile. There's the tentative expression he offered in 1952 (left, top), the confident grin under his helmet in the early 1960s (far left), and that mature, handsome smile from 1967.

The latter is a close-up taken moments after the group shot at right. The glow in the photograph is coming from four young Yankees sitting with their leader. Clockwise from lower left, that's pitcher Fritz Peterson, pitcher Dooley Womack, outfielder Bobby Murcer, and back-up catcher Frank Fernandez.

In the September 1966 *SPORT*, Sweet summed up his relationship with Mantle: "I've shot Mickey in many situations, including on a fishing boat that almost turned over. It has been intriguing watching his personality and public poise develop. The first time I worked with him he said, 'Let's hurry,' without a smile. Then, for a number of years, he said, 'Let's hurry and get it over with'— with a smile."

And it was genuine. "A real smile," says Ozzie, "is more than showing teeth. When it's real, the eyes smile."

ONES OF A KIND

Sweet caught Mantle's teammate, Roger Maris (left), in a sheepish smile framed subtly by two bat handles. This photograph dates to 1962, the year after Maris' record-breaking 61-homer season. Another Mantle pal, Billy Martin (below), managed to smile for Sweet in 1958 even though the Yankees had traded him to the Tigers. Martin was known for his aggressive style of play, his fighting, and his toughness, but he was also a useful ballplayer who was at home at second base, shortstop, or third base.

STAN THE MAN

Ozzie Sweet's portrait of Stan Musial (right) is simply one of the best in his archives. The Hall of Famer is one player who impressed Sweet both on and off the field. "I remember Musial not just because he was such a great hitter," Sweet says, "but because of his sense of style. Off the field, he dressed immaculately, with tailor-made suits and ties. He had wonderful taste; the nickname 'Stan the Man' really fit. In fact, he was a wonderful ballroom dancer. He'd enter competitions now and then— and not 'jiggity-jig' dancing, but nice waltzes, and sweeping ballroom dances."

When Sweet took the photograph shown here, Musial was in his mid-30s but still had a dangerous bat; he hit .351 in 1957 and followed with a .337 season in 1958.

"I also photographed him later in his career," Sweet recalls, "and I remember him saying, 'Ozz, what are you doing? I'm about through. Why are you photographing me?' He was flattered that I still wanted to photograph him."

A FAB FOUR

This grouping of portraits features another set of images in which Ozzie Sweet was able to nail the personalities of various players.

Good-natured Dodger hurler Don Newcombe (right) is almost laughing in his 1951 portrait. He should have been: Newcombe was 19-11 the year before, and he'd post a 20-9 record in '51.

Tony Oliva (opposite page) looks bright and hopeful in his smiling pose, which was taken after his outstanding rookie year of 1964, when he hit .323 with 32 home runs.

Joe Pepitone (below) looks brash and cocky in his portrait. Ozzie photographed the Yankee first baseman/outfielder in the mid-1960s, when Pepitone

strung together a series of productive seasons. In a four-year span starting in 1963, he hit 104 home runs.

Going back to an early-1950s portrait (bottom), Pee Wee Reese looks relaxed and confident in front of Sweet's camera.

"I always had great admiration for Pee Wee Reese for the way he made things so much easier for Jackie Robinson," says Ozzie. "He really went out of his way to help Jackie get accepted."

Reese was a true leader on the Dodgers from 1940 through 1958—an outstanding fielder at shortstop and a pesky hitter (.269, 126 home runs, 232 stolen bases) who always seemed to be on base.

"I always had great admiration for Pee Wee Reese for the way he made things so much easier for Jackie Robinson."

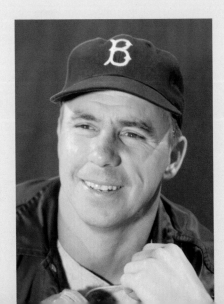

MR. ROBINSONS

Equally comfortable in sitting for Sweet were Oriole teammates Brooks Robinson and Frank Robinson; both have the "smiling eyes" that Sweet often talks about. The Robinsons joined forces, of course, when the Reds dealt Frank to Baltimore after the 1965 season. It was a shocking trade, because Reds GM Bill DeWitt gave up one of the game's true superstars while he was in his prime, reasoning that Robinson was "an old 30." In exchange, the Reds got pitchers Milt Pappas and Jack Baldschun and outfielder Dick Simpson. The trade was bad enough on its own, but DeWitt made it worse with his "old 30" comment—a barb that helped inspire Robinson to an MVP season in 1966 (.316, 49 homers, and 122 RBI).

Brooks, meanwhile, benefited from having Frank in the Orioles' lineup. The 16-time Gold Glove winner (left) hit 23 homers and drove in 100 runs in 1966, helping the Orioles to a convincing sweep over the Dodgers in the World Series.

Both Robinsons smiled for Sweet's camera in 1967, looking genuine and easygoing. The shot at right of a happy-go-lucky Robinson was taken in the early 1960s.

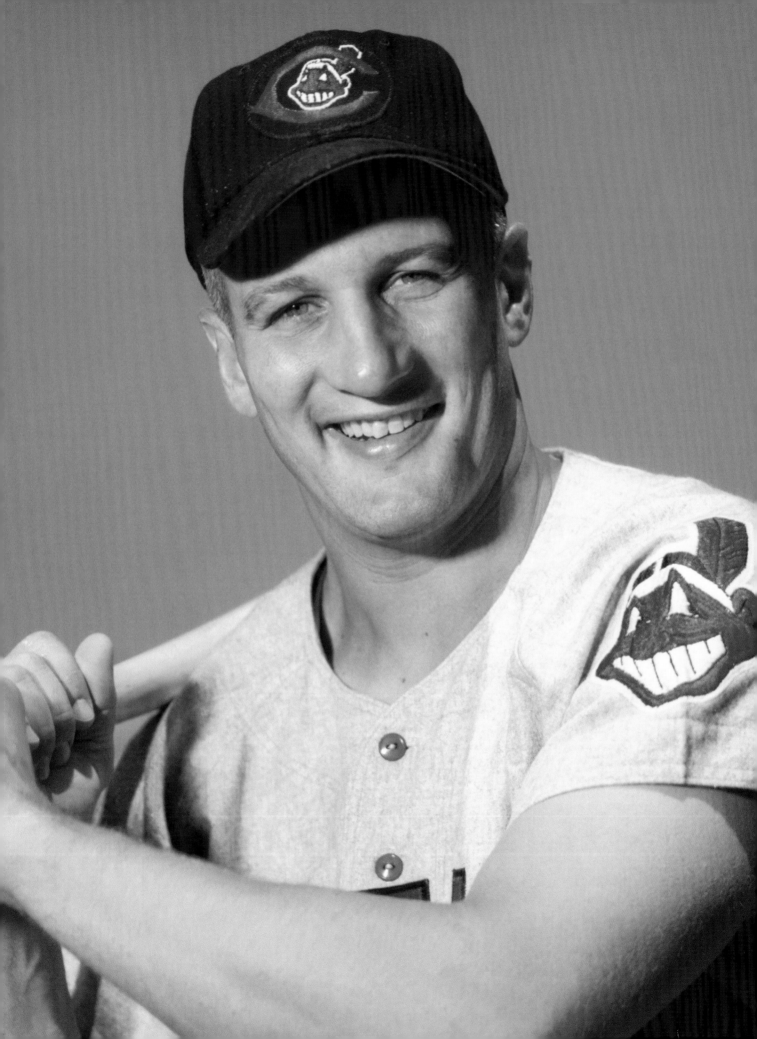

PRIME-TIME SLUGGER

Like Ralph Kiner, Al Rosen
packed a lot of power into a
short career: He played seven
full seasons and hit 192
homers. This portrait was taken
in the midst of his early-1950s
power surge (he had 37 homers
in 1950 followed by seasons of
24, 28, and 43). In posing for
Sweet, Rosen presents the
confident smile of an All-
American slugger in his prime.

SOMETHING TO CROW ABOUT

Ozzie photographed Tom Seaver
with his family at spring
training 1972 for a *Parade*
magazine cover (left). Ozzie
remembers the session well
because Seaver's young
daughter was having difficulty
sitting still for the photograph.
"So I started crowing like a
rooster," he says. "I had
perfected it pretty well,
because we had chickens on
the farm while I was growing up
and I learned how to imitate
them. So if you weren't looking
at me, you'd have thought it
was a real rooster!"

At the Mets camp that
morning, he says, "The scene
with the Seavers was so
ridiculous that the parents
laughed louder than their
daughter." With the Seavers
enjoying Sweet's "cock-a-
doodle-doos," Ozzie was able to
snag a happy portrait.

Seaver was "so pleased with
the cover," Ozzie says, "that
the following spring he posed
for a picture (above) with my
son Blair [then 14]. Afterwards,
he asked Blair if he'd like an
autographed ball—and then he
jogged around to every
teammate and had him sign it."

parade
cover photo: Nancy, Sarah and Tom Seaver
Parade's All-Star Cheering
Section of Baseball Wives
by Josh Eppinger III & Herbert Kupferberg

STAR TREATMENT

In the early 1950s, Curt Simmons and Duke Snider got the Ozzie Sweet portrait treatment. The photograph of Simmons (below), in which he's tipping his cap and offering a wide-open laugh, dates to 1952. Simmons was an "innings-eater" for the Phillies; he threw 55 complete games between 1952 and 1954, winning 44 games.

Snider (left), the Dodger slugger, gives Sweet a self-assured smile. In the early 1950s, Snider hit between 21 and 31 homers for four seasons in a row—and then in 1953 had a breakout year: 42 homers, 126 RBI, and a .336 average.

ANOTHER FAMOUS SHOT

Bobby Thomson (right) flashes an endearing "aw shucks" smile in a 1954 image. Thomson had just been acquired from the Giants, for whom he achieved baseball immortality with his pennant-clinching homer against the Dodgers in 1951. After getting traded to the Braves in 1954, he inadvertently changed baseball history again. He got hurt during spring training, opening the door for another right fielder who quickly staked his claim to the job: Henry Aaron.

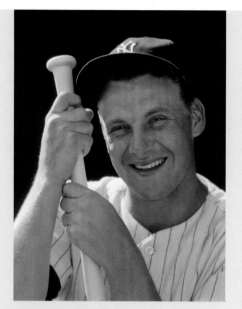

YANKEE DANDIES

The frequent championships by the Yankees in the 1950s and 1960s kept Ozzie returning to their training camp regularly. He'd photograph multiple players each time and, over the course of several years, he developed files on dozens of Yankees. Two of the team's unsung heroes were Tom Tresh (top) and Bob Turley.

Tresh was a hot property with the Yankees in the early 1960s: a switch-hitting outfielder with 25-homer power. The Tresh smile you see here dates to 1965, when he hit .279 with 26 homers.

Turley smiled for Sweet in 1956, the spring after his first year as a Yankee (he had been acquired from the Orioles). "Bullet Bob" had a 17-13 record in '55, prompting the portrait by Sweet. In 1958, he went 21-7 to win the Cy Young award.

SIMPLY SPLENDID

And finally, we have perhaps the most famous single smile of Ozzie Sweet's career: Ted Williams in that perfect portrait from 1951 (right). Williams was coming off an injury-shortened year in which he had only 334 at-bats but still hit 28 homers. But that spring, he was refreshed and ready to go, as Sweet's photograph reflects. Williams in 1951 was simply splendid, batting .318 with 30 home runs, 109 runs, and 126 RBI.

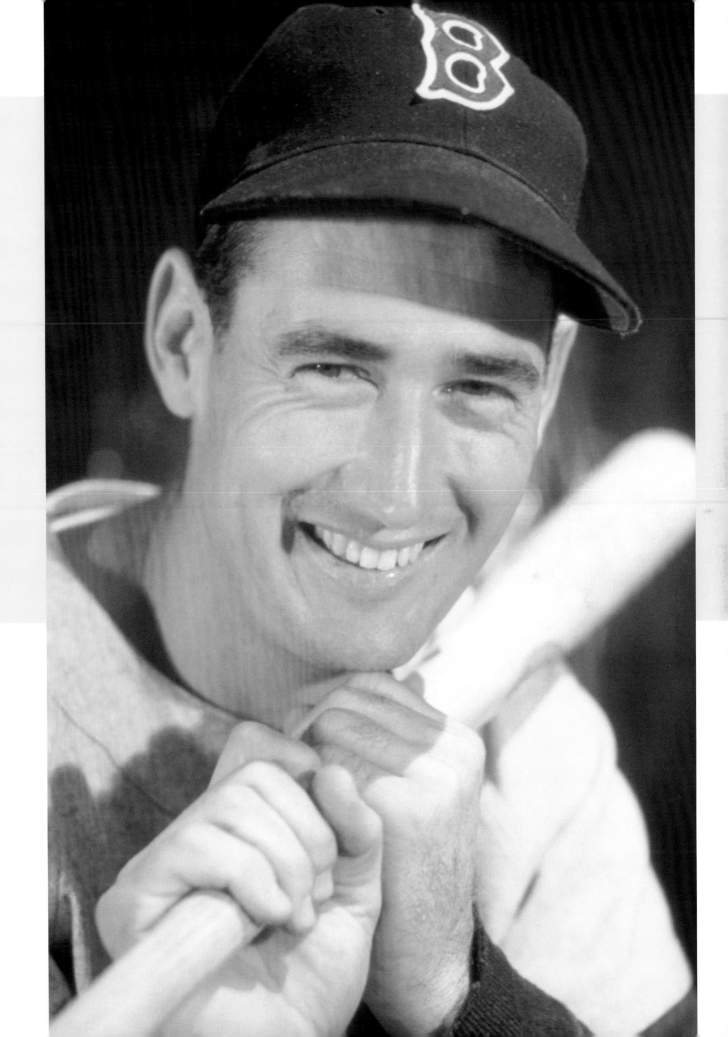

Ozzie's sense of humor shows up in this mid-1960s calendar shot. The male model is long-time assistant John Messmore. The seagull is *not* a prop.

CHAPTER FIVE

MIGHTY
WITH THE BAT

"Ozzie Sweet and Mickey Mantle had a chemistry that allowed magic to happen. Another photographer could have taken 1,000 pictures of Mickey, and they might all be good, but they wouldn't have that magic."

RANDALL SWEARINGEN

WWW.MICKEY-MANTLE.COM

Those who know Ozzie Sweet likely have heard him use the title of this chapter when he talks baseball. In discussing a player like Henry Aaron, he might say something along the lines of, "Ol' Hank sure was mighty with the bat." Or if you were to point out an obscure but promising prospect at spring training, Ozzie will try to put his potential in context by asking, "Is he someone who's mighty with the bat?"

The phrase is one you remember: "mighty with the bat." It's simplistic yet descriptive, charming yet strong. It clicks today, yet it also recalls an earlier era in baseball. And it's utterly appropriate that Sweet use the phrase, because if anyone has seen "mighty with the bat" up close and personal, it's Ozzie.

Sweet, after all, may be the only photographer who has aimed his lens at Yogi Berra as a young player in the late 1940s and Alex Rodriguez as a New York Yankee in 2005. How many men have photographed slugging outfielders from Stan Musial to Ted Williams to Willie Mays to Frank Howard to Vladimir Guerrero?

It's unlikely, too, that another photographer has captured Del Ennis, Richie Allen, and Jim Thome on film, or Ted Kluszewski, Carl Yastrzemski, and Brian Giles. Ralph Kiner was a feared slugger in the 1940s as Harmon Killebrew was in the 1960s and as Jeff Bagwell is in the 21st century; Sweet photographed them all.

In all, Sweet has photographed eight members of the 500 Home Run Club and seven others who finished with 400 homers or more, plus near-misses Al Kaline (399) and Dale Murphy (398).

THE MAGNIFICENT YANKEE

If there was one power hitter who looked naturally mighty with the bat, it was Mickey Mantle. There was something unique about Sweet's view of The Mick that gave him a larger-than-life, heroic aura. "Ozzie Sweet and Mickey Mantle had a chemistry that allowed magic to happen," says Randall Swearingen, who operates www.mickey-mantle.com. "Another photographer could have taken 1,000 pictures of Mickey, and they might all be good, but they wouldn't have that magic. "Ozzie's magic with power hitters had to do with the way he got below the waistline and shot upward," Swearingen adds. "He got these figures to look imposing, giving perspective to their forearms and shoulders. It was all in the angle Ozzie used."

Among the best examples of Sweet's mighty Mantle images is the portrait, at left. One of the most imposing portraits of Mantle ever taken by Sweet, this 1966 shot is photography as fine art (it first appeared in *SPORT* in January 1967). The low angle adds a certain drama and emphasizes Mantle's arms; it also makes his bat seem like a toothpick in his hands. If ever there was a photograph that captures the phrase "The Magnificent Yankee," this is it.

A less-threatening Mantle appears (right) in a previously unpublished photo. Sweet remembers taking this rarity during an early-1960s session.

Mantle was "in between poses," he says, "and was holding his bat in an unusual position. I took the photo at a moment when he wasn't expecting me to."

That spontaneity created an aura that's as casual as spring training itself.

THE NATURAL

The pair of memorable Mantle/Sweet collaborations on the following pages were taken some 15 years apart. The younger Mantle (left page) dates to 1952, when he was coming off an up-and-down rookie season (13 home runs in two stints with the Yankees sandwiched around a short trip to the minor leagues). The second image features the same type of pose but, somehow, Mickey looks even mightier. Maybe it's the bare arms, or the extra emphasis on his muscular torso, but there's no question that Sweet accomplished his mission here.

HAMMERIN' HANK

Hammerin' Hank Aaron was the epitome of the under-appreciated superstar, even after he went flying past Mickey Mantle on the all-time home-run list in 1969. He was remarkably steady, yet his feats were usually overshadowed by the exploits of Mantle, Mays, Sandy Koufax, and various other Yankees, Giants, and Dodgers—or by his own teammates, Eddie Mathews and Warren Spahn.

Aaron, coming off a 1963 season in which he batted .319 and led the NL in home runs (40) and RBI (130) was all business when he posed for Ozzie (top right). This classic portrait was featured in the August 1964 issue of *SPORT*.

One of Sweet's high-impact photographs of Aaron, from spring 1967, appears at the bottom of this page. "I remember taking that one," Sweet recalls. "I had Hank in a classic batting pose, looking toward the pitcher; he was cooperative, although very quiet. What I remember most is the way that big cloud rolled right into place behind him." The cloud perfectly framed Aaron's figure, helping to create a stunning photograph.

No other Aaron images from that session, unfortunately, survived the years. However, a thorough search of Sweet's archives in 2004 produced a lost treasure that had never been published: the close-up view of Aaron shown on the opposite page. For baseball fans, this one is a find—a historic look at Aaron weeks before he broke Babe Ruth's record.

Aaron finished 1973 with 713 homers, one short of Babe's 714. It was a foregone conclusion that he'd break the record early in '74. In the months leading up to the event, sadly, Aaron had to endure untold amounts of hate mail—including death threats—from racists who wanted to see Ruth's record endure. Aaron's courage was (and is) as admirable an accomplishment as his home run total. Sweet's photograph shows the effects of that pressure. "There's almost a sadness in his eyes," Sweet said shortly after rediscovering the long-lost image.

"There's almost a sadness in his eyes."

A BRAVES WORLD

By the time Aaron had his first 40-homer season (1957), teammate Eddie Mathews had already reached that level three times (1953 through '55). The lefty-hitting Mathews arrived in the Braves' lineup two seasons before Aaron and quickly established himself as a long-ball threat. He and Aaron would play together for 13 years before Mathews, after the 1966 season, was traded to Houston. He spent a half-season with the Astros and then got shipped to Detroit, where he played on the Tigers' 1968 championship team.

Mathews finished his career with 512 homers, twice leading the NL (1953 and 1959). He's the only man who played for the Boston Braves, Milwaukee Braves, and Atlanta Braves. Sweet photographed him on several occasions; in the example at right (the portrait *SPORT* used on its April 1957 cover), Ozzie had him in a pose where he looks both relaxed and, well, mighty.

Pete Rose (below) wasn't "mighty with the bat" in terms of home-run power, but he sure was effective with it. He earns his place here not only because he is baseball's all-time hits leader, but because Rose looks mighty fine in Ozzie's classic slugger's pose.

SAY HEY

In a 1998 book that ranked the 20th century's 100 greatest baseball players, *The Sporting News* put Willie Mays at No. 2, behind only Babe Ruth, and wrote, "He might have been as close to baseball perfection as we'll ever get." It's too bad ESPN's SportsCenter wasn't around in the 1950s; Mays would have been a highlight-film regular for both his offense and defense. In his 22-year career, he put up gaudy numbers (660 home runs, a .302 average, 338 steals in 441 attempts), played remarkable defense in center field (he won a dozen Gold Glove awards), and earned countless other honors (including a Rookie of the Year, two regular-season NL MVPs, and two All-Star Game MVPs).

Sweet photographed Mays frequently in the 1950s. At left, we get a great look at Mays' face in a startlingly close-up portrait taken at spring training in the 1950s.

Because Sweet was based in southern Connecticut, he'd sometimes pop in on Mays at the Polo Grounds, where the Giants played. On one such occasion, in 1954, Sweet got Mays in a vintage simulated action photograph (below). Even though it's not a spring training image, we present it here, with the following passage from Sweet's 1958 book *My Camera Pays Off*, to shed even more light on the way the photographer worked: "To get Willie Mays finishing a swing (without getting myself beaned), I rigged up an invisible piano-wire support for his bat, leaned him over a folding chair, which was hidden from the lens, and tilted my camera. Both tricks gave more of an action angle. I then shot him as he supposedly watched the ball fly over the center field wall...."

HIDDEN TREASURE

Among the National League contemporaries of Aaron, Mathews, and Mays was Roberto Clemente, the great right fielder for the Pittsburgh Pirates from 1955 through 1972. He was an all-around superstar, celebrated as much for his strong and accurate arm and his range as he was for his bat. This was an aggressive hitter who'd swing at anything: "He can hit a ball off his ankles or off his ear," Juan Marichal told *The Sporting News* in 1972. Usually, the results were positive: Clemente batted .317 with 3,000 hits and 240 homers in his 18-year career.

Clemente's career, of course, came to an abrupt end on New Year's Eve 1972, when he died in a plane crash. He was on a charity mission at the time—part of a team attempting to deliver supplies to earthquake-ravaged Nicaragua.

Sweet has fond memories of Clemente, having photographed him on several occasions. "I was always impressed with Roberto's eyes—there was so much expression in them," Ozzie recalls. "It wasn't just his intelligence; there was something special in his eyes that you usually don't see in people."

One stunning portrait from a 1970 session appears here. Sweet's technical precision and mastery of lighting resulted in a masterpiece that gives us an awesome look at Clemente's distinctive features. This wonderful image has been hidden in Sweet's archives for years.

"I was always impressed with Roberto's eyes— there was so much expression in them."

PURE POWER

For more than 10 seasons, Clemente teamed with Willie Stargell in the Pirates' lineup to give opposing pitchers headaches. They often hit back-to-back in the order—the line-drive-hitting Clemente followed by long-ball threat Stargell. In 1967, Ozzie got Stargell to strike a couple of unique poses, rubbing his hands together in a custom, raised batter's box, and striking a menacing stance in the on-deck circle. These low-angle shots make Stargell look absolutely huge.

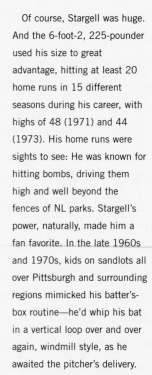

Of course, Stargell was huge. And the 6-foot-2, 225-pounder used his size to great advantage, hitting at least 20 home runs in 15 different seasons during his career, with highs of 48 (1971) and 44 (1973). His home runs were sights to see: He was known for hitting bombs, driving them high and well beyond the fences of NL parks. Stargell's power, naturally, made him a fan favorite. In the late 1960s and 1970s, kids on sandlots all over Pittsburgh and surrounding regions mimicked his batter's-box routine—he'd whip his bat in a vertical loop over and over again, windmill style, as he awaited the pitcher's delivery.

Ozzie remembers Stargell as "being pleasant and affable— truly a fun guy to be around." Stargell also became an inspiring team leader. During the Pirates' 1979 championship season, he doled out so-called "Stargell stars" to teammates in recognition of on-field achievements. After Stargell's death in 2001, the Pirates brought back the stars for the 2002 season.

FENCE BUSTER

Frank Robinson was always a willing subject for Sweet, who photographed him often because of his fence-busting feats with the Reds (1956 through '65) and the Orioles (1966 through '71). With the Reds, he had 10 straight seasons of 20 or more homers; in seven of those seasons, he had 30 or more. With the Orioles, he hit at least 25 homers in five of his six seasons. He became the only player ever to win an MVP in both leagues.

In the close-up on this page, taken in the early 1960s, the boyish Robinson is giving little hint of his power. That's in contrast to the photo on the opposite page, one of Ozzie's most effective power-hitter portraits. It shows a full-body shot of Robinson, bat cocked and ready to hit. The extremely low angle makes the Reds star look Paul Bunyanesque.

"Frank was a tough, hard-nosed guy on the field and a different person off the field—he had a ready smile," recalls Sweet.

Later in his career, Robinson played for the Dodgers, Angels, and Indians, bringing his lofty career totals to 586 homers, 2,943 hits, 204 steals, and a .294 average. During his time in Cleveland, he also became baseball's first African-American manager, taking over the team in 1975. He'd come a long way since his first season, 1956, when he hit 38 home runs and won the NL Rookie of the Year award.

"Frank was a tough, hard-nosed guy on the field and a different person off the field—he had a ready smile."

ARMED FOR ACTION

In Frank Robinson's 38-homer rookie season, two other Reds also hit 30-plus homers: Wally Post had 36 and Ted Kluszewski (pictured here) had 35. As it turned out, 1956 would be Kluszewski's last great season. He went on to play five more years but hit only 34 more homers while playing for the Reds, Pirates, White Sox, and Angels.

But if you go back to 1949, the year Big Klu became the Reds' everyday first baseman, you'll find the start of an eye-opening eight-year span. Kluszewski hit over .300 in seven of those seasons, and during one four-year stretch (1953 through 1956), he averaged .315 with 43 homers and 116 RBI per season. For a slugger, Klu had a great eye: He struck out only 140 times in 2,272 at-bats during the aforementioned four-year span—an average of just 33 times per season.

The 6-foot-2, 225-pounder was also known for trimming his shirtsleeves to show off his biceps. That quirk wasn't lost on Sweet, who made sure to play up his arms in his photographs. In these mid-1950s images, Ozzie found angles that showed off the power that sprang from Kluszewski's muscular arms.

THE BOOG BOPPER

Orioles' slugger Boog Powell was just as intimidating as Kluszewski—as we see here— with a bat in his hands.

"Boog was a massive guy— tall, husky, just big," says Ozzie. "The low angle can be really effective with that kind of subject."

This 1967 Sweet portrait puts Powell's beefy forearms front and center. And the focus is so sharp you can practically count the freckles on the big man's arms. The Baltimore first baseman was part of a high-octane Orioles offense in the 1960s and early 1970s. In a 10-year stretch from 1963 through '72, he hit 265 home runs and averaged 91 RBI per season. Late in his career he played for the Indians and Dodgers, retiring in 1977 with 339 homers.

"Boog was a massive guy—tall, husky, just big," says Ozzie. "The low angle can be really effective with that kind of subject."

BENCH-MARKS

The Reds' Johnny Bench set a new
standard for catchers with his
dominant offense and total-package
defense. He established a record for
catchers with 327 round-trippers,
and he walloped 52 more as an
outfielder, third baseman, or pinch-
hitter. He was also an innovator.

"Johnny was one of the first
catchers to wear a helmet while
behind the plate," says Ozzie. "I
really enjoyed photographing him—
there were always a lot of fun and
laughter with him."

Sweet captured Bench several
times, including this memorable
1973 shot with the catcher in his
full armor. Once again, that
patented low angle works wonders,
giving Bench an intimidating
presence. This photo appeared as a
pinup in a teen sports magazine
that summer.

MR. OCTOBER

If every superstar has a defining game, Reggie Jackson's surely came in the 1977 World Series. In Game 6, with the Yankees needing one win to clinch, Jackson came to the plate in the fourth inning and hit Burt Hooton's first pitch for a long home run. In his next at-bat, in the fifth inning against Elias Sosa, he again hit the first offering for an even longer home run. In the eighth inning, with Charlie Hough now on the mound, Jackson jumped on the first pitch and slugged it deep into the center field bleachers. Three pitches, three home runs—on a national stage.

In 1979 at spring training, Sweet's camera found Jackson in the batting cage. Like all big hitters, Jackson would draw a crowd even in batting practice. His audience in this never-before-published photograph (below) includes several Yankee stars: (from left to right) Mickey Rivers, Roy White, Chris Chambliss, Thurman Munson, whose back is turned to the camera, and Graig Nettles. (The sad epilogue to this photograph is that Munson died just five months later while flying his own plane.)

Sweet also took a notable study of Jackson, working on his swing (right), as he waited for his next turn in the cage. Of course, Jackson didn't exactly come from the Ted Williams school of disciplined, scientific hitting. Reggie had that big, all-or-nothing uppercut. Such a style tends to result in a few strikeouts, as Jackson proved. He had 2,597 Ks in his career, including 171 in 1968. But the style also produced big power numbers: In his 21 seasons, during which he played for Oakland, Baltimore, the Yankees, and California, Jackson hit 563 regular-season home runs and eight more in postseason play.

ALL THAT YAZ

Throughout his career, Reggie Jackson was a media magnet. Boston's Carl Yastrzemski was the opposite. Yaz put up impressive numbers too—but he did so in a quiet, workmanlike fashion. The hard-working, hard-hitting heir to Ted Williams took over left field at Fenway Park in 1961 and played for 23 years. His most memorable season: 1967, when his Triple Crown performance—.326, 44 homers, 121 RBI—led the "Impossible Dream" Red Sox to a thrilling AL pennant (although they fell short in the World Series). Yaz retired in 1983, at age 43, with a .285 average and 3,419 hits and 452 homers (he was the first AL player to amass 3,000 hits and 400 HRs). Late in his career, he posed for the Sweet simulated action photograph presented here.

Several years before he retired, Yastrzemski passed the left-field baton to Jim Rice, whose swing was tailor-made for Fenway Park. Rice made a career out of hitting balls over or off the "Green Monster." He was an eight-time All-Star, an MVP (1978), and a spectacular run-producer for Boston from 1975 throughout the 1980s. When he retired in 1989, Rice had a .298 average, 382 home runs, and 2,452 hits. In this portrait, taken at spring training in 1976, Rice looks powerful enough to squeeze sawdust out of his bat.

TREND SETTER

On July 5, 1947, less than three months after Jackie Robinson broke baseball's color barrier, Larry Doby got into a game with the Cleveland Indians to become the American League's first African-American player. He went on to spend eight seasons as a top slugger with the Indians before the Chicago White Sox acquired him in 1956.

Sweet, sent to photograph Doby for a *SPORT* cover that spring, put him in this playful pose, his face framed by baseballs and bats. And that smile: "A very good one—a happy one," Sweet says. "He was very interested in the big camera and tripod I was using, and he got a kick out of me getting under the dark cloth. He said he'd never been photographed that way, and he asked me all kinds of questions about the equipment. He thought it was an old-fashioned camera, and he asked if it was a valuable antique!"

The bat with all the engraved autographs is a prop that Doby himself brought. "It was a keepsake of his, a commemorative All-Star bat," Sweet recalls, "and it was his idea to use it."

UNSUNG HEROES

Certain sluggers Sweet photographed tend to get lost among the 500- and 400-homer stars in his archives. Among them are Al Rosen, Rocky Colavito, Willie Horton, Steve Garvey, and Richie Allen (all portrayed on the pages that follow). None of these long-ball-hitting legends have made the Hall of Fame, but they were stars in their own right.

Rosen played third base for the Indians in the 1950s, hitting 192 HRs in his seven full seasons. Among his best years were 1950 (37 HRs, 116 RBI) and 1953 (43 HRs, 145 RBI). Sweet captured numerous close-ups of Rosen, including the 1956 portrait presented here.

"Al Rosen struck me as a high-class sort of guy—a little more sophisticated than most ballplayers," says Ozzie.

ROCKY TIMES

After the 1956 season, Rosen suddenly retired at age 32, convinced his skills had diminished due to injuries. The same season, the Indians found replacement power in Rocco Domenico Colavito (a poetic name if ever there was one). "Rocky" hit 21 homers that year and followed it with seasons of 25, 41, and 42 homers. In 1960, Cleveland dealt him to Detroit, where he'd spend four years, including his best season (1961, when he had 45 HRs and 140 RBIs). In 1959, Ozzie tracked down Colavito for a portrait and the result was an eye-catcher, or, for Rocky, an eye-popper.

*"I'd tell him some of my one-liners,
and he'd laugh hard and long."*

Colavito's early-1960s stint
with the Tigers overlapped with
Willie Horton's career by one
season. Willie was in Detroit for
a short spell in 1963 and again
in 1964. He won the left-field
job in 1965, and from that
point through 1976, he
averaged 22 homers per year,
with a high of 36 during the
Tigers' 1968 championship
season.

In the photograph on the
opposite page, Sweet captured
Horton's stocky, sturdy build in
a 1971 full-body batting pose.
Horton's upper-body strength
was evident in the close-up
below. Ozzie also captured
Horton's work ethic in the
batting cage.

"He looks serious here, but
Willie Horton used to smile and
laugh a lot while I was setting
up," recalls Ozzie. "I'd tell him
some of my one-liners, and he'd
laugh hard and long."

SURLY SLUGGER

The year Horton made it to the majors, 1963, was also the year that Richie Allen debuted. Allen came up for the proverbial cup of coffee with the Phillies that season and returned to stay in 1964, winning Rookie of the Year honors with a .318, 29-HR, 91-RBI season. For the next 10 years, he was one of baseball's steadiest sluggers, averaging 29 homers a season. Ozzie photographed the versatile Allen (he played first base, third, and outfield) in his prime in the mid-1960s. On the opposite page he's a picture of confidence in a classic hands-on-hip pose. At left, Ozzie's close-up, straight-on shot gives you a sense of the intimidating view that greeted NL pitchers of the 1960s.

Allen's image as a malcontent may have overshadowed his hitting ability: He went from Philadelphia to St. Louis in 1970, Los Angeles in 1971, the White Sox in 1972, Philadelphia (again) in 1975, and Oakland in 1976. But the man could hit: He retired as a career .292 hitter with 351 homers, seven All-Star appearances, and the 1972 AL MVP award, when his 37 HRs and 113 RBI led the league.

"When Roger arrived, he was very amused by the setup."

BATMEN

Alex Rodriguez looks confident and powerful in posing for this March 2005 portrait. He was also reverent toward the cameraman: Afterwards, he said he was "excited and honored to be photographed by Ozzie." He also noted that "you don't see portraits like [Ozzie's] shot anymore." Baseball fans don't see many players like A-Rod: In 11 seasons through 2004, he had 381 homers, a .305 average, 1,096 RBI, an MVP award, and three home run titles.

A-Rod follows in the footsteps of a great number of "mighty" Yankees, including Roger Maris, who may have been cool toward the press but who always found time for Ozzie. In this famous shot, Sweet patiently suspended several baseball bats with string and persuaded Maris—fresh off his record-breaking 61-homer season, to play along. "When Roger arrived, he was very amused by the setup," recalls Sweet. The result was magic.

CHAPTER SIX

MOUND MAGIC

"Certain people are heroes, and Sandy Koufax is one of my heroes."

OZZIE

Here's another impossible-looking Ozzie Sweet photograph taken with his custom-built semi-sub. There's no Photoshop work here: Ozzie's lens is shooting above and below water at the same time.

Photographing big, burly hitters wielding a club is one thing: You go for that powerful, imposing look. What about pitchers? Well, Ozzie Sweet, in his work for *SPORT* magazine in the 1940s through the 1970s, handled them individually, depending on their attributes, skills, and personalities.

Consider Sandy Koufax. The Dodgers' lefty wasn't a loud, rah-rah type of guy; rather, he was quiet, focused, and resolute, a professional—so he should look that way, Sweet figured. And his portraits accomplished just that. Even though Ozzie loved Koufax's smile— "even his eyes would be sparkling"—he usually presented Koufax as a serious, determined competitor, as illustrated on these pages.

The image below is a startlingly true photograph, beautifully lit, with impeccable detail (see his No. 32 inked on Koufax's glove). The photo at left is a brilliant study in detail, between the sweat stains underneath the bill of his cap, and the texture of his hat. This photograph was used on the September 1965 *SPORT* cover.

Koufax was one of Ozzie's favorite players.

"Certain people are heroes, and Sandy Koufax is one of my heroes," says Ozzie. "I photographed him on several occasions, and he could be a little moody: One time he might have been jolly and happy and everything was fine, while the next time, I could tell something was bugging him. But even then he was cooperative."

To capture the grandeur of Koufax, Ozzie liked to shoot him from a low angle.

"I'd have him on a platform propped up by sawhorses so I could shoot from below the level of the ground. Not many photographers did that; I don't remember ever seeing one build a stage to represent the pitcher's mound. But it allowed me to get in there and photograph him from a low angle, and to show what he looked like in his windup."

Koufax retired after the 1966 season at 30, an age when pitchers usually are in the midst of their most productive years. Despite his early exit, brought on by an arthritic left elbow, he was in the Hall of Fame on his first try, getting elected in 1971 and inducted in 1972. His accomplishments included a 165-87 record, a 2.76 ERA, an MVP award (1963), and three Cy Young Awards (1963, '65, '66). "I have great respect and admiration for the guy," says Ozzie. "My experiences with Sandy were always great. He was always on time for our shoots, and he'd listen and understand what we were doing."

THE INTIMIDATOR

Right-hander Don Drysdale made it to the Dodgers the year after Koufax did but found more immediate success. In his second season, 1957, he went 17-9 with a 2.69 ERA. He would post double-figure win totals for each of the next 11 seasons, with his best years coming in 1962, when he won the Cy Young Award on the strength of his 25-9 record and 2.83 ERA, and 1965, when he was 23-12 with a 2.77 ERA. In 1968, Drysdale threw 58.7 consecutive shutout innings, a record that stood for 20 years. He could hit, too, slugging 29 career home runs, including seven in 1965, when he batted .300 in 130 at-bats.

One of the most intimidating pitchers of his era, Drysdale was a tall (6 feet, 6 inches), imposing fellow who owned the inside part of the plate. He hit 154 batters in his 14-year career and knocked down countless others. Like Koufax, Drysdale retired early due to arm woes, ending his career after the 1969 season at age 32, finishing with a 209-166 record and a 2.95 ERA.

Appropriately, Sweet coerced a look of toughness from Drysdale in one of his best portraits of the pitcher; it's presented on the opposite page. His eyes hint at the fierceness with which he pitched. As you'd expect, the detail in this photograph, which dates to 1962, is tack-sharp: the

piercing eyes, the buttons on his jersey, the "air holes" under his arms....

Eight years before he took the Drysdale photograph, Sweet put Dodger pitcher Carl Erskine in a follow-through pose (top, right). Erskine was coming off his finest season: 20-6 with 16 complete games and four shutouts in 1953. In his 12 years with Brooklyn and Los Angeles (the Dodgers having moved west in 1958), Erskine had a .610 winning percentage, a record of 122-78, and an ERA of 4.00, throwing two no-hitters along the way.

In 1946, the Yankees sent power-hitting second baseman Joe Gordon and infielder Eddie Bockman to the Indians for pitcher Allie Reynolds (bottom). Cleveland got four quality seasons out of Gordon (he hit 29, 32, 20, and 19 homers in that span) and the Yankees got an ace. Reynolds was barely a .500 pitcher with Cleveland, going 51-47 from 1942 through 1946. But in his first year in New York, he was 19-8 and won another game in the World Series. He would pitch eight years for the Yankees, posting a 131-60 record.

Reynolds' best year was 1952, when he was 20-8 with a 2.06 ERA. That spring, Ozzie took several portraits of "Superchief," one of which appears here—a straight-on shot that defines Reynolds: nothing fancy, just reliable and solid.

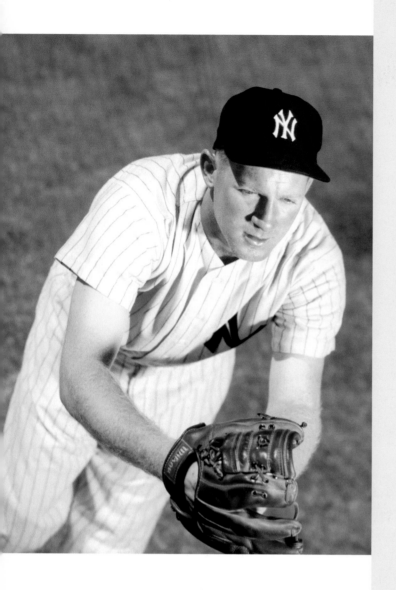

MIGHTY WHITEY

In Allie Reynolds' last two seasons with the Yankees, 1953 and '54, he spent more time as a reliever than as a starter. One of the reasons was the emergence of Whitey Ford. After posting a 51-20 record in three and a half minor-league seasons, the young lefty debuted in the majors in 1950. He made the most of his chance, winning nine of 10 decisions in 1950, but missed the 1951 and '52 seasons while serving in the military. Upon returning in '53, he picked up where he left off, going 18-6. It was the first of 13 straight winning seasons by Ford. He was equally effective in postseason play, compiling 10 World Series wins and a 2.71 ERA in 22 starts.

Ford retired in 1967 with a record of 236-106 and a .690 winning percentage (sixth-best in baseball history). Along the way, he worked with Sweet on several occasions, including a mid-1950s session that produced the images here. For the top photograph, Ozzie took a different tact than usual, shooting from above rather than below. This portrait gives us a great view of the detail in Ford's glove and the look of sheer concentration in his eyes. The image below is a more casual, somewhat endearing take: Ford with his hands on his hips, his glove looped around his wrist.

RAPID ROBERT FELLER

The first baseball player Ozzie photographed at spring training was Bob Feller, back in 1947. That assignment was for *Newsweek*; two years later, Sweet was again framing Feller in his lens, this time for *SPORT*. One of the results appears here: a 1949 close-up portrait of the square-jawed pitcher tipping his cap.

"Sometimes, I'd take Bob Feller or his teammates outside of the ballpark in Tucson to photograph them," recalls Ozzie. "I'd say to them, 'Could you guys come out here in the desert?' There's nothing out there—it made for a clean background, nothing but blue sky."

Feller was the Indians' ace from the late 1930s (he was 17 when he debuted in the majors) through the early 1950s. The reason *Newsweek* featured him on a 1947 cover was because of his dominant pitching in 1946: a 26-15 record, 36 complete games, 10 shutouts, and a 2.15 ERA. It was the fourth time he'd won at least 24 games in a season, and he was only 27—and remember that he missed nearly four seasons because of military duty. In fact, "Rapid Robert" would have won 300 games easily if not for his service time. As it is, he had a 266-162 record with 2,581 strikeouts and a 3.25 ERA.

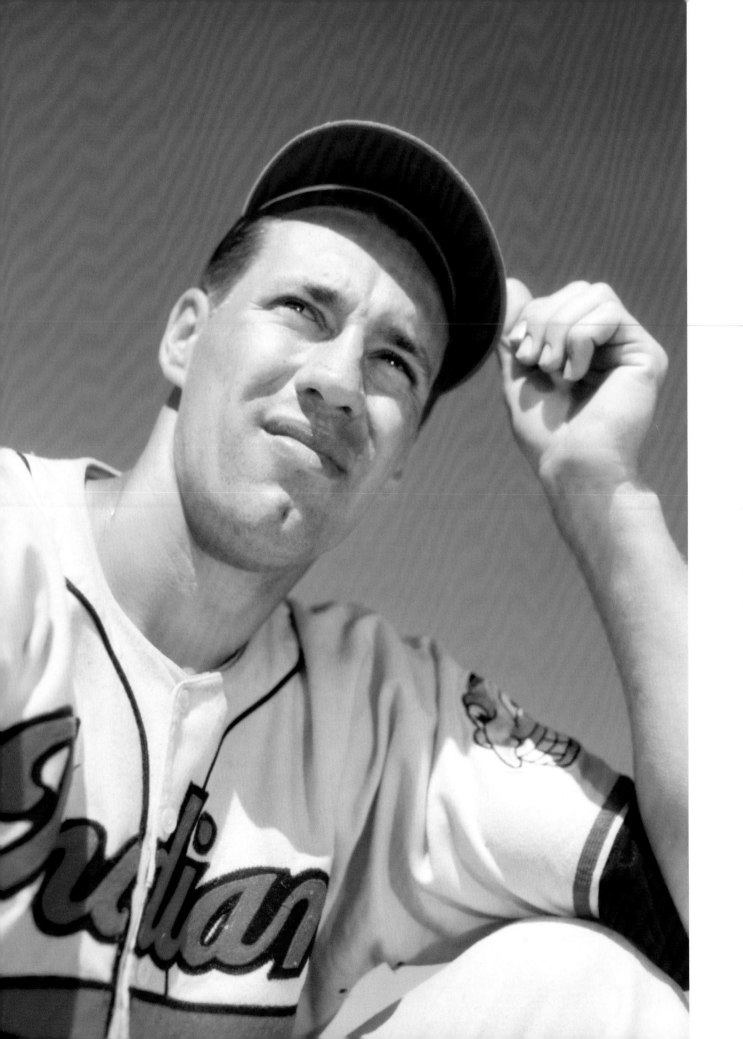

A PAIR OF ACES

During Feller's peak years of the late 1940s and early 1950s, the Indians boasted two other ace-quality hurlers: Bob Lemon and Mike Garcia.

Lemon got to the majors in 1946 at a fairly late age (at least compared to Feller): 25. Two years later, he was a 20-game winner. In fact, Lemon won 20 games seven times in a nine-year stretch (1948 through 1956). He also was a key to the Indians' 1948 world championship, winning both of his starts in the World Series and allowing only three runs in 16.3 innings. His career numbers: 207-128 and a 3.23 ERA.

Lemon twice appeared on the cover of *SPORT*: June 1950 and May 1953. The former cover shot is presented on the opposite page, a wonderfully angled photograph of Lemon leaning in toward the catcher, a baseball visible behind his back. (Note the Indians' logo; years later, it would become the subject of controversy, understandably so, when it drew the ire of Native Americans.)

As for Garcia, he twice led the AL in ERA (1949 and 1954) and twice won 20 games. His best season: 1952, when he finished at 22-11 with six shutouts and a 2.37 ERA. He retired with a 142-97 record and a 3.27 ERA. In the early 1950s, Sweet photographed Garcia several times; the sessions produced *SPORT's* September 1952 cover as well as the portrait presented here.

PHILLIE FIREPOWER

At times, Sweet would call on teammates to pose together; a prime example appears below. In this fun photograph, which dates to 1951, Phillies' pitcher Jim Konstanty shares a secret with Robin Roberts.

Konstanty was a highly regarded relief pitcher who was so effective in 1950 that he won the NL MVP award. He had a 16-7 record and a 2.66 ERA that season, pitching 152 innings and allowing only 108 hits. Saves weren't an official statistic back then, but if they had been, Konstanty would have been credited with 22.

Roberts also joined the Phillies in 1948 and quickly became an ace. The right-hander won at least 20 games six years in a row (1950 through 1955), including his remarkable 28-7, 2.59 season in 1953. He was a true workhorse, leading the NL in innings pitched every year from 1951 through 1955.

We see a candid view of Roberts at right. In that one, a Sweet grab of the 1955 Phillies training camp, Roberts is swinging a bat—something he did well that season, for a pitcher: He batted .252 with a pair of homers in 107 at-bats. Also in the photograph are Marv Blalock (No. 47), Fred Van Dusen (No. 45), and Stan Lopata (No. 29) of the Phils and Gus Bell (No. 25) of the Reds.

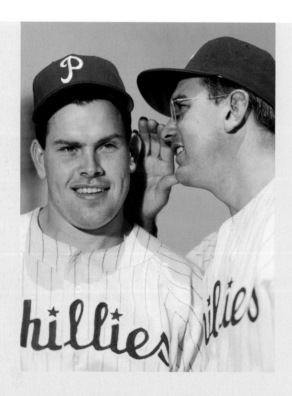

A WHIZ KID

The 1950s-era Phillies also boasted a tough lefty in Curt Simmons. A highly regarded pitcher as a teenager, Simmons signed with Philadelphia in 1947 for a then-exorbitant $65,000. By 1950, he had become a reliable starter, posting a 17-8 record for the NL champion "Whiz Kids." He won 79 games over the next six seasons, earning a spot on the NL All-Star team three times in that span. Sweet's pitching-pose portrait of Simmons (left) dates to 1952.

Jim Bunning was a model of consistency in four seasons with the Phillies, winning 19, 19, 19 and 17 games from 1964-67. The future member of the U.S. Senate, who won 224 games in his career, struck a serious pose for Ozzie (below) in 1965.

LEFTY EXTRAORDINAIRE

In the mid-1960s, Steve Carlton's fastball, scouts thought, would keep him from becoming a major league pitcher. "Lefty" proved them wrong, pitching for 24 years, winning 20 games six times, earning All-Star honors nine times, and winning four NL Cy Young awards.

Sweet photographed Carlton in spring 1971 for a May 8, 1971 cover story in *The Sporting News*. The magazine used a smiling portrait, but Sweet also captured Carlton looking sullen (the unpublished photograph seen here). It's understandable if he were a bit dispirited: Carlton was coming off a season in which he was snake-bitten, suffering through a 10-19 record despite a respectable ERA (3.73). In 1971, he found his groove, compiling a 20-9 record and a 3.56 ERA. He was even better in 1972, winning 27 games with a 1.97 ERA and 310 strikeouts in 346 innings.

KING OF THE HILL

Steve Carlton won 329 games, second among lefties only to Warren Spahn, captured here in a straightforward, startlingly close portrait by Sweet.

Longevity was a key to Spahn's pitching record: He played 21 years even though he got a late start due to military service. Spahn didn't win his first game until he was 25 (in 1946), but from that point on, the Ws piled up quickly. He won at least 20 games 13 times in a 17-year span (1947 through 1963), leading the NL in wins eight times and in ERA three times.

Spahn kept pitching until he was 44, ending his career with the Mets and Giants in 1965. His final tally: a 363-245 record (only five pitchers in MLB history had more wins), a 3.09 ERA, 382 complete games, and 63 shutouts.

TRADE TALK

The Detroit Tigers pulled off a headline-grabbing deal following the 1970 season. They sent pitchers Denny McLain and Norm McRae, outfielder Elliott Maddox, and infielder Don Wert to the Washington Senators for pitchers Joe Coleman and Jim Hannan, third baseman Aurelio Rodriguez, and shortstop Eddie Brinkman.

In spring 1971, before the "results" were in on the big trade, Ozzie visited both the Tigers' and Senators' camps. At Pompano Beach, Fla., he captured not only the images of Ted Williams that appear in Chapter 3, but this striking wide-angle look at McLain in his windup. Over in Lakeland, where the Tigers were training, Sweet took a low-angle portrait of Coleman in a pitching pose (bottom left) and also grabbed a photograph of Coleman and Rodriguez returning to the Tigers' bench after retiring the side in a spring training game. (That's Deron Johnson of the Phillies partially hidden behind Rodriguez.)

The trade, of course, turned out to be a major heist on the part of the Tigers. Hannan didn't last long in Detroit, but Rodriguez and Brinkman steadied the left side of the Tigers' infield and Coleman became a stud on the mound for several years. McLain, meanwhile, couldn't have pitched much worse for the Senators, winning only 10 games and losing 22 in '71. It would be his only season with the franchise.

WARMING UP
Closer to the parking lot than the infield, unidentified members of the Pirates were spotted loosening up in the bullpen in this 1980 Ozzie shot.

Among Ozzie's Florida assignments was to shoot close-up portraits for romance magazine covers in the late 1950s and early 1960s.

CHAPTER SEVEN

NICKNAMES AND FACES

"In baseball, more than any other sport, nicknames seem to stand out. They add a certain color, or flair, to our favorite players and to the game itself."

OZZIE

Sports fans today know Chris Berman, the popular ESPN announcer, for the creative nicknames he's been bestowing upon athletes since the early 1980s. Tom "Leave It To" Seaver. Glenn "Old Mother" Hubbard. Julio "Won't You Take Me on a Sea" Cruz. Marty "Grin and" Barrett. Bert "Be Home" Blyleven. Ballplayers and nicknames, after all, fit together like the seventh-inning stretch and *Take Me Out to the Ballgame.*

Going back to the late 19th and early 20th centuries, we find plenty of colorful nicknames. It's hard to think of Willie Keeler—the 140-pounds outfielder who hit .341 during his 19-year career—without instinctively putting the "Wee" in front of his first name. Fred Merkle was anointed "Bonehead" after his base-running mistake cost the New York Giants a pennant in 1908. Mordecai Brown, who won 239 games in pitching from 1903 through 1916, was more widely known as "Three-Finger" Brown, a moniker stemming to an accident when he was 7. (Working on his uncle's farm, his hand got caught in a corn grinder, which took off almost his entire forefinger and mangled his middle finger.)

And the biggest stars of baseball's early days always seemed to have a nickname. Ty Cobb, "The Georgia Peach." "The Big Train," Walter Johnson. Walter "Rabbit" Maranville. "Shoeless" Joe Jackson. Lou Gehrig, "The Iron Horse." Jay Hanna "Dizzy" Dean. Some had multiple nicknames, among them George Herman Ruth—"The Babe," "The Bambino," and "The Sultan of Swat."

Clever nicknames aren't lost on Ozzie Sweet, whose photography often reflects his sense of humor. "In baseball, more than any other sport, nicknames seem to stand out," Ozzie notes. "They add a certain color, or flair, to our favorite players and to the game itself." The player Sweet photographed more than any other, Mickey Mantle, was tagged "The Commerce Comet" early in his career because of the town where he grew up (Commerce, Okla.) and his blazing speed. He photographed Willie Mays, "The Say-Hey Kid"—a catchphrase that reflected his enthusiasm for the game. He photographed Ted Williams— "Teddy Ballgame," or "The Splendid Splinter."

His camera also captured, among many others, the images of Mudcat Grant, Hideki "Godzilla" Matsui, Bucky Dent, and "Charlie Hustle" Pete Rose, to name a few of the faces that appear on the pages that follow.

DRIFTWOOD KING

Hall of Famer Clarence Vance (known to all by his nickname, Dazzy) retired to Florida in 1935 and, as a hobby, collected driftwood. Ozzie got Dazzy to display some of his wares in this striking 1950s pose.

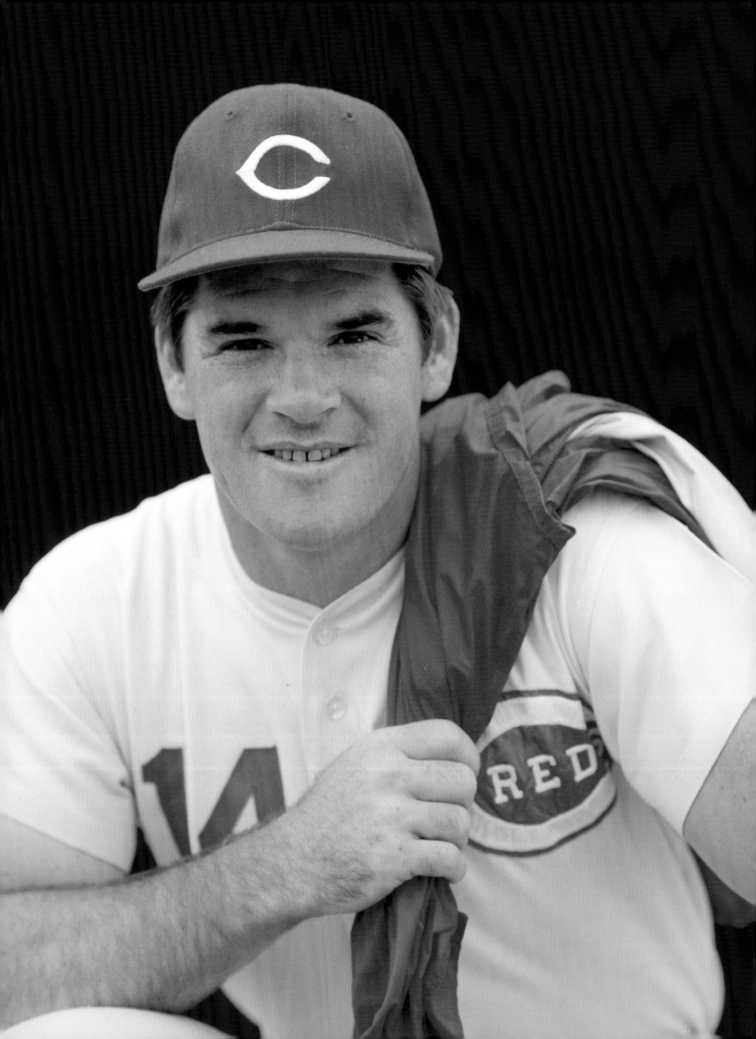

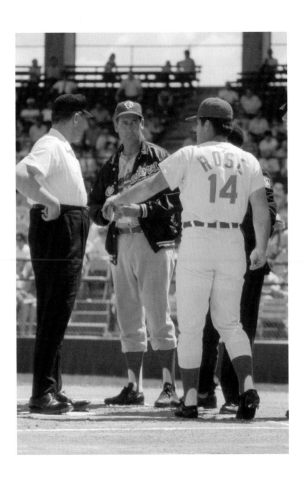

CHARLIE HUSTLE

Pete Rose got his nickname, as the legend goes, from Whitey Ford after the great Yankee pitcher saw, during spring training, the way he'd sprint to first base after drawing a walk. Ford was not being complimentary. In the end, though, the nickname stuck—and it said volumes about the way Rose played. He didn't have the natural ability of a Mantle or Mays, but he made up for it with his all-out hustle in digging and scratching and line-driving his way to the all-time hit record. It was 1985 when Rose broke Cobb's mark of 4,189 hits. At the time, Pete was the Reds' player/manager, having been reacquired by his original team after five years with the Phillies and a partial season with the Expos.

Fifteen years earlier, Sweet got "Charlie Hustle" to slow down long enough to pose for a striking set of portraits, including the one pictured on the opposite page. "I didn't get a lot of photographs of Pete smiling," remembers Ozzie. "Even here, you can tell that he just didn't smile very easily."

Sweet also captured Rose in a series of 1971 spring training candids, several of which appear here for the first time. Most notable is an image where Rose—reviewing ground rules with an umpiring crew before a Senators/Reds spring training game—gets a look of consternation from Ted Williams (left). "Ted sure looks impatient, and maybe a little irritated, doesn't he?" Sweet says. "He doesn't seem open to hearing what Rose has to say."

In another candid (bottom), Ozzie captures Rose "working" an umpire—during a spring training game! Even in pre-season contests, Rose looked for any advantage he could get. The ump seems to be gesturing, "You were out by this much, Pete!"

"Even here, you can tell that he just didn't smile very easily."

Rose would play a key role on two Cincinnati "Big Red Machine" championship teams (1975 and 1976). After the 1978 season, at age 37, he became a free agent and signed with Philadelphia. And two years later, in 1980, he helped the Phillies win their first-ever World Series, ending nearly 100 years of frustration.

The following spring, 1981, Sweet photographed Rose with the Phillies, getting this particularly tight candid of Rose deep in thought. (That's outfielder Garry Maddox in the background.) Rose looks like he's analyzing a teammate's swing. At the time, he was developing an interest in managing; he'd get his shot

less than four years after this image was taken. From 1985 through 1988, Rose would lead the Reds to four straight second-place finishes before dropping to fifth place in his last season as a manager, 1989. That was the year he was banned from baseball over gambling charges.

THE COBRA

Among the other well-nicknamed players in Ozzie's archives is Dave Parker, "The Cobra." Early in his career, which began in 1973 in Pittsburgh, the big left-handed hitter appeared headed for the Hall of Fame. He hit over .300 in each of his first five full seasons and won an MVP award in 1978, when he continued playing even after incurring a broken jaw. He had one of his best all-around years in '78: a .334 average, 30 HRs, and 117 RBI.

In the early 1980s, injuries combined with bouts of excessive weight and drug abuse sent Parker into a tailspin and took away the speed in his cobra-like swing. Only after a 1984 trade to Cincinnati—where he played for Pete Rose—did he regain his form. Parker played until the age of 40, putting in time with the A's, Brewers, Angels, and Blue Jays in his final four seasons and finishing with 339 HRs, 2,712 hits, and a .290 average.

Shown here are two Sweet views of Parker in 1980. At left, we see him after hitting a home run in a spring training game against St. Louis, accepting congrats from teammates Tim Foli and Bill Robinson. (That's All-Star catcher Ted Simmons behind the plate for the Cardinals.) Below is a dugout candid of Parker picking out a pair of shades while sitting on the Pirates' bench next to Dale Berra, Yogi's son.

DR. STRANGEGLOVE

A Pirate player from an earlier era, Dick Stuart (above), had a far less complimentary nickname than Parker's: He was known as "Dr. Strangeglove." Stuart could hit, as he proved with Pittsburgh in 1961 (.301 with 35 HRs) and the Red Sox in 1963 (42 HRs, 118 RBI) and 1964 (33 HRs, 114 RBI). But, to put it mildly, he was never a Gold Glove candidate.

Playing first base, Stuart averaged 20 errors a year between 1958 and 1965. During one span, he led NL first basemen in errors five seasons in a row, tying a record. Obviously, "Dr. Strangeglove" was born about 15 years too early: The designated hitter rule didn't come into play until 1973.

LE GRAND ORANGE

A nickname like "Le Grand Orange" can mean only one thing: a large man with orange hair. Well, it sure beats "Big Red."

Actually, Daniel Joseph Staub already had a nickname, Rusty, well before arriving in the majors. It was during his stint with the Montreal Expos that he received the more stately "Le Grand Orange."

The Expos snagged Staub in the 1968 expansion draft after the Houston Astros left him unprotected. He hit 29 and then 30 home runs in his first two years with the Expos, followed by a 19-HR, 97-RBI, .311 performance in 1971. He earned All-Star honors for five consecutive seasons.

Despite Staub's popularity in Montreal, the talent-hungry Expos traded him to the Mets in 1972, receiving Ken Singleton, Tim Foli, and Mike Jorgensen in return. Staub spent four seasons in The Big

Apple, with his best numbers coming in 1975 (.282, 19 HRs, 105 RBI). Again, though, he found himself on the trading block. The Mets sent him in 1976 to the Tigers in the ill-fated deal for Mickey Lolich, who went 8-13 in his only season in New York.

Ozzie photographed Staub in 1976 at the Tigers' training camp and produced the striking hat-over-the-heart portrait presented below—a variation of his classic Roberto Clemente image from 1970. At right is a candid that exudes spring training atmosphere: a bird's-eye view of Staub and Bill Freehan during infield practice, taking ground balls at first base. Staub looks somewhat amused as Freehan—a longtime catcher near the end of his career—focused on the next grounder.

Another player in Ozzie's archives who was nicknamed for a physical trait is Ron Cey. Teammates called him "Penguin" because of his short, stocky legs and his choppy, side-to-side running style. Forget his physique; the man could hit. In his 17 seasons (12 with the Dodgers, starting in 1971), he hit 316 homers, drove in 1,139 runs, and batted .261. Ozzie's close-up of Cey (left) dates to the early 1980s. Cey looks to be showing off his famous legs to Ozzie (bottom left), but in fact he's just loosening up.

Ozzie's portrait of Dusty Baker (below) dates to his early-1980s years with L.A. He also played for the Braves, Giants, and A's, hitting 242 homers.

GODZILLA!

Hideki Matsui earned the nickname "Godzilla" for the way he terrified pitchers as a schoolboy in Japan: He hit a record 60 home runs in his high school years. In 1993, he joined the Yomiuri Giants and went on to blast 332 homers in 10 seasons. Godzilla has hit 47 more HRs in his first two seasons as a Yankee. The monstrous nickname doesn't fool Ozzie Sweet, however: After photographing Matsui in 2003, '04, and (at right) '05, the words Sweet uses to describe him are "polite," "gentle," and "respectful."

MUDCAT

Mudcat Grant was a hard-throwing pitcher who played for seven teams between 1958 and 1971. His best year came in 1965, when his 21-7 record helped put Minnesota into the World Series. Grant beat L.A. in Game 1, lost Game 4 and won Game 6, hitting a three-run homer in the process. The Dodgers would win the Series in seven games. The following spring, Ozzie took the portrait of Grant shown above. Mudcat, by the way, got his nickname at his first spring training. It was 1958 at the Indians' camp, and his teammates thought he hailed from Mississippi, a "mudcat state" (he's actually from Florida). They noticed, as Grant once told a reporter, "that I always had mud on my shoes when I came into the clubhouse," so they called him a variety of names, including "Mudman" and "Mudshoes." But it was "Mudcat" that stuck.

BATTLING BILLY

As a player, Billy Martin was known as "Billy the Kid" for his hard-nosed style and sheer toughness. As a manager, he became "Battling Billy." He was a Yankee for his first six and a half seasons, finally getting traded to Detroit after a much-publicized nightclub brawl.

"I photographed Billy quite a bit, and he was very easy to work with," says Ozzie. "I know he could get ticked off and swear a little, but not with me. He always laughed a lot and was even a bit mischievous."

The Ozzie view of Martin at left finds Billy during his only spring training with the Tigers, 1958. Ozzie also caught up with Billy (far left) when he was managing the Rangers in 1975, and the Yankees (above).

199

Bucky Dent's place in baseball history is set in stone, thanks to the dramatic (and unlikely) three-run homer he hit to save the day during the Yankees' 1978 one-game playoff win over the Red Sox. At the time, it was one more argument for "The Curse of the Bambino." The following spring, Ozzie took a tight candid of Dent (left) at the Yankees' camp in Ft. Lauderdale, Fla.

Saturnino Orestes Armas Minoso, known as Minnie Minoso (bottom), is known for playing in the major leagues in a record five decades. He came up with the Indians in 1949, starred for the White Sox and Indians in the 1950s and early 1960s (he also spent a year in St. Louis and another with the Senators), and came back to pinch-hit for the White Sox in 1976 (at age 53) and again in 1980 (age 57).

Then there was Vinegar Bend Mizell (right), a pitcher who won 68 games for the Cardinals between 1952 and 1959 (he later pitched for the Pirates and Mets). Mizell's given name was Wilmer David. So where'd his nickname originate? He was born in an Alabama town called Vinegar Bend.

SIMPLY SANGY

Some nicknames are simply shortened-up last names: not very creative but easy to remember. Roy Campanella was "Campy," Willie McCovey was "Mac," and Carl Yastrzemski was "Yaz," for example. And Manny Sanguillen, the Pirates' longtime catcher, was known to his teammates as "Sangy."

Sanguillen was one of baseball's happiest souls during his playing days—always smiling and upbeat. He was a notorious bad-ball hitter, but he did it effectively, batting .296 in his career. Ozzie photographed Sangy in the early 1970s, getting him in a tight close-up (left) wearing a catcher's mask, and also in a simulated action shot (far left) where he tore off his mask, obviously to pursue one of Ozzie's imaginary pop-ups.

Here's one of Ozzie's "sweet" setups, created for a calendar in the 1970s.

CHAPTER EIGHT

RETURN OF THE MASTER

"Even in his 80s, he can still execute a clear, individualistic vision and style. I tend to think of Ozzie more as an artist, maybe a pop artist."

MARK DURAND

ESPN CLASSIC

In 2005, Ozzie Sweet returned to spring training at age 86 to continue photographing a new generation of stars. A year earlier, he had visited five camps in five days, and in 2003 he hit four training sites in four days. And four years before that, he went to the Yankees' camp to photograph a trio of sluggers. To Sweet, none of this was a big deal because he'd done it so many times in the past. But to everyone who knows him or knows of him, Sweet's most recent trips are "amazing": They highlight the man's longevity, his accomplishments, his eye for a photograph, and his perfectionism.

Sweet's first spring training session was in 1947. Think about that. Harry Truman was president, John F. Kennedy was five years away from his first senatorial election win, and Bill Clinton and George W. Bush were not yet a year old. *The Diary of Anne Frank* was published in 1947. Nolan Ryan, Johnny Bench, and Carlton Fisk were born that year; so were Billy Crystal, Elton John, and David Letterman. In 1947, Babe Ruth was still alive, and Casey Stengel was two years away from getting hired as the Yankees' manager. The first polio vaccine was six years in the future, and the first Frisbee was 10 years away. Up until the 1947 season, African-Americans were not allowed to play major league baseball. And television was still somewhat of an exotic box at the time; in fact, it was September 1947 when the World Series showed up on TV for the first time.

Yet here was Sweet in March 1947, at age 28 already a top magazine cover photographer, arriving at the Indians' camp in Tucson in search of Bob Feller. That single session would set Sweet on a path from which he would make an indelible mark in sports portraiture.

In the 1950s, as ESPN Classic's Mark Durand says, "we didn't see our heroes in color very much. But Ozzie's photos were always in color, and they had a heroic quality. When you're a kid, you haven't really ingested your sports heroes as real people yet. Ozzie's photographs had a sort of fanciful quality—he made it easy for us to see them as icons. His images were like Greek mythology; the players seemed larger than life. Yet at the same time, his photographs had a Hollywood quality, kind of like the movies do. Definitely, he's made an important contribution to sports history."

"If Sinatra has been the soundtrack of our lives, Ozzie's work has been the portraiture of our baseball lives," says author, historian, TV producer, and former Yankees' publicist Marty Appel. "There was a time when every boy's room was decorated with full-page 'Ozzies,' so distinct in their look. Before color TV, he gave us the stars of the game up close and personal, and the fact that he continues to do so enriches our appreciation of his work and his subjects. He's the DiMaggio of his craft; he makes it look easy when, in fact, there were none like him."

In 2003, '04, and '05, nearly six decades after his landmark Feller session, Sweet proved he's anything but the retiring type. In fact, he's never thought about retiring. Even after cutting back on baseball photography in the mid-1980s, he continued to work at a full-time pace, stopping only for occasional setbacks (like hip replacement surgery in 2000). He focuses mainly on vintage automobiles these days, and he also "makes photographs," as he says, for a series of calendars featuring kittens and puppies (he's always been fond of animals, domestic and otherwise).

But when Sweet does return to the diamond, it's a special occasion for anyone lucky enough to watch him work his magic: fellow photographers, managers and coaches who remember his work in *SPORT*, players who have a keen awareness of baseball history, and legions of fans from the old days, some of whom are now in a position to expose his photography to the masses.

"The fact that he's still doing it is amazing," says Durand, who—in his role as director of program development for ESPN Original Entertainment and ESPN Classic—has used numerous Sweet photographs in biographies and documentaries. "Even in his 80s, he can still execute a clear, individualistic vision and style. I tend to think of Ozzie more as an artist, maybe a pop artist. And with any artist—a painter, a writer, a musician—what makes them distinctive is that you know their work just by looking at it; you can identify them by their style.

(Continued on Page 209)

STILL GOING

That's Ozzie, above, in the white shirt and cap beside the Pirates' batting cage in 2003, doing what he does best, and at right, focussing on a stretching Pirate.

"All in all," Sweet says, "spring training is
even more interesting now than it was
years ago. There's so much more going
on now, so much more to photograph."

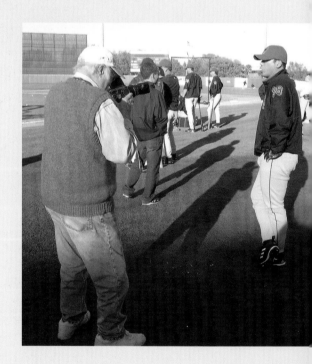

"Ozzie's always had his own style, and he still has it," Durand adds. "That stubbornness and tenacity to get things right the old way is what makes him special. The artistic sensibility that he's long had—people respond to that. Ozzie is more interested in the story of a picture than he is in capturing the realism of something. That's not very typical today, outside of certain types of photographers who do totally artistic shooting. Richard Avedon has his style, and Ozzie Sweet has his style. His way of shooting pictures has always been very distinctive and recognizable."

The images that made Sweet most famous were his patented simulated action photographs. In 2003 and '04, however, he decided to forego that elaborate process; instead, he says, "I wanted to record spring training as it looks today—the players, the parks, the routines, the atmosphere."

So he focused on taking candid studies of players along with grabs of anything that says "spring training"—from the media, crowds, groundskeepers, and batboys to ballpark architecture and landscapes. "All in all," Sweet says, "spring training is even more interesting now than it was years ago. There's so much more going on now, so much more to photograph."

And what's it like to watch Sweet work at spring training these days? Well, he'll tell you with a smile that he doesn't move around as quickly as he used to. But there's no question he still has an eye for picking spots—sights that he knows will produce high-impact photographs. And there's no question he enjoyed himself every step of the way on his recent tours, both for the satisfaction of knowing he's "still got it" (as one photographer put it) and for the inevitable nostalgia rush he felt.

"The tours brought back all kinds of memories," Sweet says. "In many ways, we're treated at the ballparks just as nicely as we were years ago. It was similar to the old days, although it takes a little longer to get what you need because the media demand is so much greater. Back then, there wasn't this battery of photographers armed with those big, long lenses. There were maybe a dozen of us."

Another difference between then and now is Sweet's own celebrity. He attracted enough attention at camp in 2003, '04 and '05 that, to his surprise, he became the subject of several newspaper and television features. "Back in the old days," he says, "I was just another working photographer."

Even more gratifying to Sweet, however, was the attention he received from today's photographers. At every camp, at least two or three top lensmen approached him—almost in awe (and quite surprised that he's still active)—to express their appreciation for his work.

Rich Pilling, Major League Baseball's director of photography, told Sweet, "You're the reason I got into this line of work." Pilling's nonstop studying of Ozzie's *SPORT* portraits as a kid, he said, sparked his desire to become a photographer. "Ozzie is absolutely a pioneer in color sports photography and an inspiration to me," Pilling says.

Victor Baldizon, a freelancer whose images have appeared in books as well as such magazines as *Sports Illustrated* and *ESPN: The Magazine*, told Sweet, "You have no idea how many people you've touched with your photography. I just want to say thank you." Longtime *Sports Illustrated* photographer Chuck Solomon also talked about the way he was drawn into his career by the impact of Sweet's classic photographs. So did Steve Moore, who shoots action as well as Ozzie-inspired portraits for top magazines and newspapers, and Larry Kinker, a top baseball photographer for Fleer, and John Soo Hoo, the Dodgers' team photographer.

Time and again on the tour, Sweet was reminded of the fraternity of which he's long been a part: "Photographers really look out for each other," he says. "And it's always been that way."

MODERN-DAY OZZIE: A TRAVELOGUE

Times may have changed since the 1940s, but Ozzie Sweet's penchant for crisp, colorful images has not, as his recent spring training photos show. While his images speak for themselves, it would be impossible for a writer (namely, me) to go on such an excursion without documenting it. Here's the city-by-city account.

HEART OF THE YANKEES
Ozzie's trip to the Yankees' Legends Field in Tampa in March 1999 was his first training-camp visit in some 10 years. He arrived to photograph Paul O'Neill, Bernie Williams, and Tino Martinez for a magazine assignment. The previous year, the trio led the Yankees to a world championship. Williams won the AL batting title with a .339 average and also had 26 homers and 97 RBI. O'Neill hit .317 with 24 homers and 116 RBI, while Martinez hit .281 with 28 homers and 123 RBI.

Sweet wanted to line up the sluggers in their batting stances and shoot from his patented low angle. His only requests were a baseball diamond (he was directed to an unused practice field) and a flatbed trailer on which the three players could stand to allow Sweet to shoot from below. The result (right) was the heart of the Yankees' order: from left, Tino Martinez, Bernie Williams and Paul O'Neill.

"The 1999 Yankees session was a huge thrill," says Ozzie. "Like years before, I couldn't waste time, so I had everything planned out in advance, and I had to be limber and work quickly. It made me feel young again."

On the next page, Ozzie kept the same order intact in a more relaxed pose. On page 213, Ozzie got O'Neill to take a knee (top), captured a larger-than-life Williams (middle), and got Martinez to strike a signature Ozzie stance (bottom).

A longtime Sweet assistant, John Messmore, was on hand to help. Today a successful entrepreneur, Messmore met Ozzie in the early 1950s when he modeled for a photo shoot at age 11. In the years that followed, he regularly assisted Sweet at spring training; one of his main jobs: "flash-bulb changer." Messmore would quickly unscrew the scalding-hot bulbs and replace them with new ones ("Ozzie was often ready to take the next image while I was still putting new bulbs in place," he says).

"I was amazed at how gentle and persuasive Ozzie was," Messmore recalls. "He was sincere—and not in a manipulative way. After all, you can't fool those guys [the ballplayers]. With Ozzie, it was almost like he was there to give something, not to get something."

Rejoining Sweet in 1999, Messmore discovered some things never change. Just like in the old days, Ozzie's sessions went smoothly "because of his nature, his positive attitude," says Messmore. "I like to call him 'unconsciously confident.' He knew he'd get what he needed; the word 'failure' is simply not in his vocabulary."

"The 1999 Yankees session was a huge thrill...
It made me feel young again."

"I was amazed at how gentle and persuasive Sweet was," Messmore recalls. "He was sincere—and not in a manipulative way. After all, you can't fool those guys [the ballplayers]."

"This isn't the Cadillac or Lincoln of cameras, it's the Rolls Royce"

JIM DANDY

In mid-March 2003, Ozzie left his coastal Maine home for the warmth of the Florida sun, ready to add a chapter to this book—and to his career. First stop: the Astros' home, Osceola County Stadium in Kissimmee. The Phillies were in town for a pre-season contest and Sweet arrived three hours before game time. The only people around: a few players milling about and a couple of media members doing the same.

After the Phillies filed onto the field to loosen up, Jim Thome agreed to pose for "Mr. Sweet." But first, he said, "Wait a minute—I've gotta get somebody." He turned and jogged over to a young teammate and then brought him back, saying, "I'd like Jim here in the picture too, if you don't mind." Jim Crowell is a strapping minor-league pitcher. Thome (left) and Crowell offered friendly smiles while Ozzie took several images using his favored Hasselblad ("This isn't the Cadillac or Lincoln of cameras," he says, "it's the Rolls Royce").

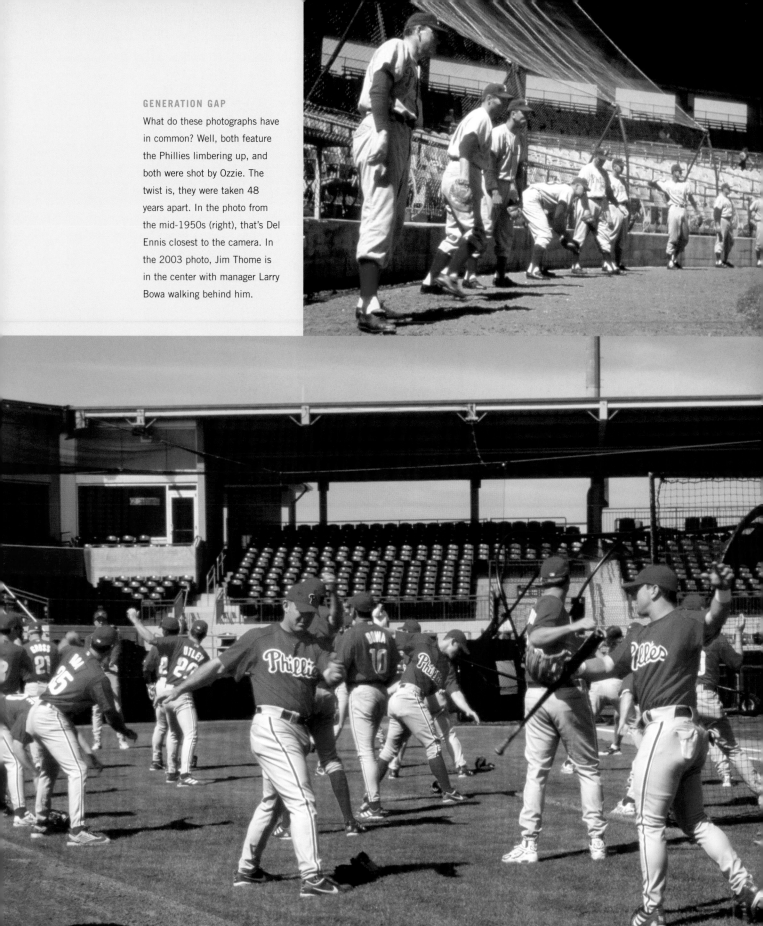

GENERATION GAP

What do these photographs have in common? Well, both feature the Phillies limbering up, and both were shot by Ozzie. The twist is, they were taken 48 years apart. In the photo from the mid-1950s (right), that's Del Ennis closest to the camera. In the 2003 photo, Jim Thome is in the center with manager Larry Bowa walking behind him.

PART OF THE JOB
During batting practice, Sweet spotted Philadelphia's Pat Burrell leaning against the cage and moved in for a close-up, capturing the outfielder wearing a pensive expression as he studied a teammate's swing. Later, Burrell looked more at ease as he conducted a television interview.

DOWN AND DIRTY

Jeff Bagwell, as spring-training-watchers know, sometimes leaves preseason games after three or four innings, walks to a practice field, and takes extra hitting. Sure enough, on the day that Ozzie was in town, the first baseman came out of the lineup in the fourth inning, headed down the left-field line, cut over to an adjacent field, and began a BP session (right). After some 45 minutes of practicing his stroke, Bagwell gathered his bat, towel, and water bottle and headed out. First, though, he agreed to pose—but said: "I should probably go get cleaned up." Sweet said no, he liked what he saw. And so he fired away, capturing a strikingly honest photograph (below) that forever fixes the dirt, sweat, and sun of spring training onto Bagwell's face.

MOVING ON

After photographing Bagwell, we left Kissimmee for Montreal's camp in Viera, a 75-minute drive. The facility in Viera was new to the Expos; the Florida Marlins trained there up until 2002 (in fact, the seats in Space Coast Stadium retain the Marlins' bright teal color). Sweet's main objective was to catch up with Frank Robinson. The Expos' manager, however, was holed up in a private coaches' meeting all morning, so Sweet grabbed a variety of other scenes, including this atmospheric shot of the Expos' pitching staff holding an early morning, on-field meeting.

STAR POWER

Vladimir Guerrero, the multi-talented outfielder, smiled for Sweet before stepping into the cage for BP in 2003. It was his final Expos training camp. Guerrero played out the final year of his contract with the Expos in 2003—batting .330 with 25 home runs in just 394 at-bats—and signed with the Angels. In the AL in 2004, he picked up where he left off, winning the MVP award with a spectacular .337, 39-homer, 126-RBI season.

ALL SMILES

With still no sign of Frank Robinson, Ozzie persuaded Jeff Liefer (left) to give him a smile. Then the visiting Mets started to arrive and Ozzie spotted the engaging smile of outfielder Tsuyoshi Shinjo. Ozzie got him to hold his bat just right (above) and captured an image that highlights the delight of spring training. Finally, Robinson arrived. Ten minutes before game time, Robby and Ozzie took a few minutes to renew acquaintances before Ozzie shot the photograph that appears on Page 10. These few moments sent Ozzie's mind racing back to the mid-1960s, when he captured Robinson, then a young Reds' star, with his view camera on several occasions.

PRIDE OF THE PIRATES

After leaving the Expos' camp, we drove three hours west to Bradenton, where the Pirates train at McKechnie Field, a wonderfully nostalgic park dating to 1923. In 2003, the team's top performer was Brian Giles, a hard-hitting outfielder who averaged 37 home runs a season from 1999 through 2002. Sweet arranged to photograph Giles (right) in a "throwback" pose—a low-angle view of the slugger in his stance, bat in hand, forearms filling the frame in an image that could only be Ozzie's. He also got a candid of Giles being interviewed, plus two shots of him stretching with a team trainer.

Giles, as it turned out, didn't last with the Pirates through the 2003 season. In the final year of a contract, he found himself shipped to San Diego in August in return for outfielder Jason Bay (who won the 2004 NL Rookie of the Year award) and pitcher Oliver Perez.

GODZILLA MEETS OZZIE
Ozzie's next destination was Legends Field in Tampa. Even at spring training, the Yankees pull swarms of press members; interest was at an all-time high in 2003 because of the arrival of "Godzilla," Hideki Matsui, from Japan. Publicity director Rick Cerrone conducted special meetings on procedures for the Japanese media, who showed up to follow Matsui's every move. Matsui, stretching, is oblivious to all the camera lenses trained on him.

THE MANAGER

When Matsui stepped into the batting cage, he got special attention from manager Joe Torre (below), who was able to watch over all his hitters from a perch right behind the batting cage.

Far removed from the Matsui madness, a lineup of Yankee pitchers (right) warmed up at a practice field next to Legends. The big lefthander is David Wells; next to him is Mariano Rivera.

GIAMBI BROTHERS

Yankee first baseman Jason Giambi was enjoying a fun spring in 2003. He was coming off a monster 41-homer, 122-RBI, .314 season (and, of course, his steroid-abuse controversy was still some 18 months away). On this spring morning, a team from the YES Network had erected a portable studio (top) and spent the morning waiting for Giambi. They waited until around 4 p.m. before Giambi (middle photo) finally broke loose from his workouts.

Meantime, the Red Sox were in town, and Giambi's brother Jeremy (bottom) was in camp. He paused for Ozzie during batting practice for a serious-faced candid—perhaps a harbinger of things to come: Jeremy suffered through an injury-plagued .197 year, and was released after the season.

THE EARLY BIRD

Before the players arrived at Legends Field in Tampa, the grounds received a manicure from a lone groundskeeper. Among the few witnesses to his work was Ozzie, who created this serene image of a ballpark coming to life in the morning.

Ozzie's 2004 tour started off at the Astros' camp in Kissimmee, where the Mets were visiting. During the off-season, Houston signed ex-Yankee pitchers Roger Clemens and Andy Pettitte; Sweet was eager to photograph both. While waiting for the dynamic duo, he came away with all kinds of gems.

Sweet noticed Mets manager Art Howe (left), in his final season with the Mets, presenting a striking square-jawed profile as he watched his players hit. Astros manager Jimy Williams (below) struck a more serious pose as he stood in the dugout with his coaches for the national anthem. Williams would be fired 88 games into the season and Howe in mid-September.

JUST LIKE EINSTEIN

Outfielder Lance Berkman (above) of the Astros, coming off a 25 home-run and 93-RBI season (and heading into a 30-105 year in 2004), was happy to pause for an Ozzie portrait. Berkman, then 28, was one of the few modern players familiar with Ozzie's work, and even thanked Ozzie for photographing him.

Meanwhile, Mets outfielder Mike Cameron trotted in from the outfield to take his swings, but took a moment to pose for what he thought would be a fairly serious study by Sweet. Ozzie looks for smiles, so I tried to coax one from Cameron by saying, "In Ozzie's early years, he actually photographed Albert Einstein. That puts you in pretty good company, don't you think?" Cameron flashed a broad grin, and Sweet captured the moment.

With game time approaching, Clemens and Pettitte, unfortunately, never left the Astros' off-limits workout facility. No matter. One of Sweet's most admirable traits is his ability to shrug off disappointments. He preferred to focus on the day's successes—or at least what he speculated would be successes. "Even now, after all these years, I still get nervous when I send transparencies out for processing," he says.

LEAPIN' MAURY

Day 2 on the 2004 tour brought a moment Sweet had been waiting for: a return to Vero Beach, where the Dodgers train. In the 1950s and 1960s, Ozzie grew fond of "Dodgertown"; in fact, he often used his favorite beachfront hotel in Vero Beach, the Driftwood Inn, as his headquarters during extended stays in Florida.

On this sunny spring morning in 2004, Sweet walked into Holman Stadium, with its unique uncovered dugouts, and took a long, wistful look around the park. He could almost see the ghosts of himself as an energetic, enthusiastic 28-year-old photographer working with Jackie Robinson on this very field in 1949. He recalled the spot where he posed Sandy Koufax at the start of his windup in a 1963 session. And he remembered a mid-1960s image he produced in which Maury Wills appears to fly through the air, directly over the top of the photographer (right). Sweet created that effect by lying on the ground, in a slightly sunken gully, and having Wills leap over him.

Maury Wills, in fact, is here today—some 40 years after he last saw Sweet. He took a break from the bunting drills he's conducting to say hello. "I was honored to be in your book, Ozzie," he says, referring to 1993's *Legends of the Field.* "Thanks for getting me in there." We tell him we're hoping to photograph him in that same pose—the leaping one. "You're not getting me up in the air like that again!" Wills says with a laugh. But he does pause for Ozzie, resulting in the closeup (bottom) below, placed beneath a close-up shot from some 40 years ago.

CANDID CAMERA

After reminiscing with Wills, Ozzie captured several more Dodger images: Paul LoDuca (top right) and Dave Roberts (bottom right) talking to the media; and a close up of Shawn Green lost in thought. The Dodgers traded LoDuca to the Marlins and Roberts to the Red Sox in mid-season. Roberts went on to become a 2004 playoff hero during Boston's unforgettable championship. Green was traded to Arizona in early 2005.

229

TWO OF THE BEST

His stop at Vero Beach allowed Ozzie to photograph two all-time great managers: former Dodger skipper Tommy Lasorda and Cardinals manager Tony LaRussa (right). That's Lasorda (below) sitting in the back row on the Dodgers bench behind current manager Jim Tracy. Pitching coach Jim Colborn is wearing No. 48 and infielder Jolbert Cabrera is wearing No. 6.

Just before the national anthem was to begin, Sweet exited the playing field near the L.A. dugout and landed in an empty seat in Row 1. Sitting in Row 2: new Dodgers owners Frank and Jamie McCourt, who two months earlier had their $430 million acquisition of the team approved by Major League Baseball. The McCourts struck up a conversation with Sweet and—obviously familiar with his work—complimented him on his career. They also asked if he'd do the honor of taking their family's portrait.

AU REVOIR

After a day at Vero Beach, we headed to nearby Viera on a trip to what turned out to be the final camp in the Expos' history. Encountering his old friend, Frank Robinson, Ozzie got off some shots of Robinson looking quite managerial (left), and seemingly unworried about the state of the franchise, which would relocate to Washington as the Nationals in 2005.

Ozzie also ran into freelance photographer Baldizon, a longtime fan of Sweet's work. Baldizon had become friends with the Expos' talented double-play duo, Orlando Cabrera and Jose Vidro, so he asked them to "pose for Mr. Sweet," describing to them in Spanish the impact of Ozzie's photography. Both cooperated willingly, allowing Ozzie to capture Vidro (below) in a reflective mood.

MAGICAL WORLD

The next day's destination might be described as the polar opposite of decades-old Dodgertown: Disney World, where the Atlanta Braves train.

During Sweet's heyday with *SPORT*, Disney World was a mere concept; construction didn't begin until 1969. Today, the sprawling theme park includes Disney's Wide World of Sports complex. On this warm March morning, the Braves were preparing to host the Yankees, who arrived in Orlando minus Derek Jeter and newly acquired Alex Rodriguez. Sweet was unfazed by the absence of those megastars; instead, he focused on the way the sun seems to light up the grass, the crowd, and the colors of Cracker Jacks Stadium.

As the Braves loosened up to play the Yankees, Sweet scoped out potential photographs, finding one in manager Bobby Cox, who was laughing with former teammate Bobby Murcer (above, left), now a Yankees announcer. Ozzie also zeroed in on 25-year-old Marcus Giles (above, brother of Brian Giles) and 45-year-old veteran Julio Franco (right), a spring training regular since 1979.

CATCHING UP

When the Braves finished batting practice, the visiting Yankees emerged and prepared to hit. Ozzie noticed that his old friend Yogi Berra had traveled with the team that day and was sitting on the bench giving an interview. Sweet subtly slid in front of Yogi and captured him on film for the first time since the 1980s. When the two started reminiscing, Ozzie mentioned that he'd be turning 86 in a few months. Berra, who at the time was 79, replied, "Well, I'm gonna catch up to you... I hope."

Shown here is an Ozzie portrait of Yogi from the 1950s (below) and a pair of shots from 2004. Their encounter reminded Sweet of a favorite moment in the 1950s: "One year, I photographed Yogi as if he'd just taken off his catcher's mask and had thrown it out of the way. I had the mask hanging there from fishing leader, off of a crossbar, with Yogi posed in front of it. Imagine how silly that looked. A few of his teammates came by and started to tease Yogi, but he yelled back to them, 'Hey, don't bother us! Ozzie knows what he's doing!' I always liked Yogi for that.

"It was great fun to see him again," Sweet added. "He looks the same as he did when I photographed him 20, 30, 40 years ago. There's very little difference."

"A few of his teammates came by and started to tease Yogi, but he yelled back to them, 'Hey, don't bother us! Ozzie knows what he's doing!' I always liked Yogi for that. "

YANKEE STARS

When the Yankees began loosening up, coach Don Mattingly walked by and agreed, reluctantly, to pose with a couple of bats over his shoulder. Clearly his heart wasn't in it: "Donnie Baseball," who in 2004 was a first-year coach, made an attempt to smile and then rushed off to work with a hitter. Sweet shrugged: "That was a waste of film...."

But within a few minutes, the photo ops start coming. Hideki Matsui (top), waiting his turn to hit, agreed to give Ozzie a few moments and is caught eyeing the camera. Sweet then spotted Gary Sheffield (left) signing autographs for an enthusiastic cluster of fans. We've seen this type of photograph before, but on Ozzie's film, it's somehow different: His composition shows us exactly what it feels like to get besieged with a flurry of long-armed autograph requests.

"OL' CASEY USED TO SIT BACK AMONGST A GROUP OF WRITERS AND TALK AND TALK."

DÉJÀ VU

The pairing of photographs at left helps put Ozzie's longevity in context: candid grabs of Yankee manager Casey Stengel (top) looking over his team in 1949 and Joe Torre doing the same 55 years later, in 2004. Equally amazing, more than 40 years after Ozzie captured Stengel talking to the media (below), he found Torre doing likewise in 2004, speaking to Pete Van Wieren, longtime Atlanta Braves play-by-play announcer.

"Ol' Casey used to sit back amongst a group of writers and talk and talk," Sweet recalls. "As a photographer, you were far enough away that you didn't quite know what he was saying, but you'd hear these continuous bursts of laughter."

LIKE FATHER...

Sweet's five-day 2004 tour concluded in St. Petersburg, where the Tigers were visiting the Devil Rays. Detroit's newly acquired All-Star catcher, Ivan Rodriguez, was there with his 11-year-old son Dereck. Sweet instantly envisioned a father/son image, so we made a request. A reluctant Rodriguez said, "Not right now. Maybe in a while..."

Ozzie focused on a variety of other images—including one shot of Rodriguez (right) waiting to take batting practice—but figured the father/son opportunity had passed. Then Rodriguez suddenly reappeared and said, "I'm ready; can you do it now?" Ozzie quickly posed father and son, asking them to show the 7s on their backs.

Later, we learned that *Sports Illustrated* photographer Chuck Solomon delivered an assist. Upon learning of I-Rod's evasiveness, Solomon privately prodded the catcher: "Come on—this is the Babe Ruth of photographers! Give him five minutes..."

The I-Rod success more than balanced a Devil Ray snub late in the day. Outfielder Rocco Baldelli took more time explaining why he couldn't cooperate than he would have spent if he had just smiled for Ozzie's camera. But, hey, even the real Babe Ruth didn't hit a home run every time.

PROUD IN PINSTRIPES

When 2005 arrived, Ozzie was back at spring training, shooting for *Sports Illustrated*. Among the results: a striking portrait of Randy Johnson (above), the 6-foot-10 lefty who became even more imposing with Sweet's low-angle view. "He has that 'mean' look down pat, with those glaring eyes," Sweet chuckled.

Ozzie also captured "the manager and the captain," Joe Torre and Derek Jeter (right), and Bernie Williams stretching (top right). Torre showed up and deadpanned, "Okay, you've got exactly one minute." He then gave Ozzie a half-hour.

And Jeter? "Photographing Derek compares to photographing Mickey Mantle or Ted Williams—it's the same thing, the same aura," Sweet says. "He's got that star quality, and he wears it well."

BEANTOWN BOMBERS

Baseball's biggest story in 2004 was Boston's first World Series title since 1918—the year Ozzie Sweet was born. Fittingly, Sweet finished his 2005 tour by photographing the champions on two consecutive days. First, he caught the Red Sox at the Twins' spring training complex in Lee County. Among the sights: manager Terry Francona (top) giving reporters some quotable pre-game tidbits. Later, he took a long view of slugger David Ortiz picking up where he left off in 2004: hitting a grand slam against the Twins. That's Ortiz (left) about to cross home plate.

The next day, at Boston's spring training home in Fort Myers, Sweet captured pitcher Tim Wakefield (above) showing a Japanese TV crew how to throw a knuckleball. He also took some stunningly close portraits (right) of Jason Varitek. The catcher's rugged style of play and steady leadership prompted the Boston brass to anoint him captain before the '05 season—only the third player (joining Carl Yastrzemski and Jim Rice) to receive the honor since 1923.

THE CATALYST

Finally, what better way to finish than with a smiling Johnny Damon? Boston's charismatic catalyst lets it all hang out on the field—and off, too. His style—and his style of play—attracted a cult following of fans, "Damon's Disciples," who showed up at games wearing white robes, wigs, and fake beards. He didn't disappoint, batting .304 with 123 runs during the '04 season and hitting two key homers, including a grand slam, in Boston's win over the Yankees in Game 7 of the AL Championship series.

To Ozzie, Damon is "as good a camera subject as he is a ballplayer. He has a wonderful, ready smile that looks genuine because it is genuine."

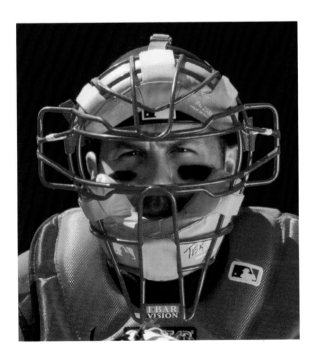

239